On This Day In
WYOMING
HISTORY

PATRICK T. HOLSCHER

THE
History
PRESS

Published by The History Press
Charleston, SC 29403
www.historypress.net

First published 2014

Manufactured in the United States

ISBN 978.1.62619.223.2

Library of Congress CIP data applied for.

CONTENTS

ACKNOWLEDGEMENTS

This book has been a long project in many ways and, indeed, started in vague ways years ago. A lot of people deserve credit, therefore, for helping me with it. A lot of those people I will have forgotten to include in one way or another, for which I hope they forgive me.

More than anyone else, I want to thank my family—my wife, Darcie; son, Marcus; and daughter, Alexis—for the role they have played in this project. They've been hauled along on numerous side trips and sometimes inspired them. And the topics in here have formed the table talk, sometimes against their wills, at numerous meals and gatherings.

I'd also like to thank my parents, Patricia and Thomas, for inspiring in me a love of history. And thanks to my friends Todd Holmes, Mark Johnson, Lyndon Couvallion, Rick Throckmorton, Joe Sullivan and Phillip Saulerlender, who have carried on many conversations on history topics with me. Finally, I'd like to thank Becky LeJeune, of The History Press, for her patience while I was continually late on forwarding material for this book.

INTRODUCTION

This book is the byproduct of a blog that I started more or less two years ago, in which I have attempted to catalogue Wyoming's daily history on a day-by-day basis—or at least that's how the writing of the book commenced. Many of the entries found here first appeared in the blog. The desire to write a history of Wyoming, however, dates back much further than that, and that desire remains one that has not yet seen itself in print. This work is, in some ways, the starter on that.

Beyond that, this text somewhat had its origins in a thread on the forum site for the Society of the Military Horse, an organization that explores the military use of equines. A long-running thread there, which I had been updating for some time, explored that topic on a daily basis. In the process of doing that, I began to incorporate items from Wyoming's history. I started to note, in doing that, that there really wasn't any one synthesis for Wyoming's history on a daily basis, so I went out to create one. You now have that work in text form. I hope that you find it useful and enjoyable. It doesn't, of course, list everything that happened in Wyoming on any one day, which would be something like an encyclopedia. Rather, it hits topics that are large, amusing or sometimes simply national in scope but that had a significant impact on the state.

It no doubt will find fault with some and be less complete than some may like. Any introductory work of this type is going to have those problems. Nonetheless, I hope that it proves to be a useful and enjoyable book for the reader. Beyond that, hopefully it'll convey a sense of the state that it's about and its history and culture.

JANUARY IN WYOMING

January is a very cold month in Wyoming, with average temperatures falling in the five- to ten-degree range. The month is generally cold but not necessarily snowy, although the snow that falls in the high country generally remains until spring. In a very cold year, snow can remain at lower elevations as well, keeping in mind that Wyoming has a fairly high elevation overall.

For this reason, activities in the state at this time of year historically have tended to reflect the cold weather, occasionally in odd ways. At one time, for example, ranching activities were at a low at this time of year, and for that reason the legislature's start was set in January, where it remains. Also, during the nineteenth century, some winter Indian campaigns were conducted by the U.S. Army, as the native peoples were very constricted in movement during this month of the year.

For those who enjoy the winter sports, however, it's a month that provides opportunities, albeit cold ones. Skiing, snowshoeing, waterfowling and snowmobiling are common January pursuits.

January 1—New Year's Day

1863 Daniel Freeman files the first homestead under the newly passed Homestead Act. The homestead was filed in Nebraska.

A Nebraska homestead of a type common on the Plains everywhere. While the original Homestead Act provided an unsuitably small portion of land for those wishing to homestead in Wyoming, it was used here, and it can be argued that homesteading was responsible for defining the modern character of the state. *Library of Congress.*

1870 Carbon County comes into existence.

1918 Oil and gas pipeline commences operation from the Salt Creek field to Casper. It is the first such pipeline in the Casper region.

1930 Fort D.A. Russell becomes Fort Francis E. Warren. The post remains open today as Warren Air Force Base.

1934 Joseph C. O'Mahoney takes office as a Democratic senator from Wyoming. O'Mahoney was born in Chelsea, Massachusetts, in 1884 and entered the newspaper business as a young man as a reporter. He relocated to Boulder, Colorado, in 1908 and then, in 1916, to Cheyenne, where he became the editor of the *Cheyenne State Leader*. He apparently

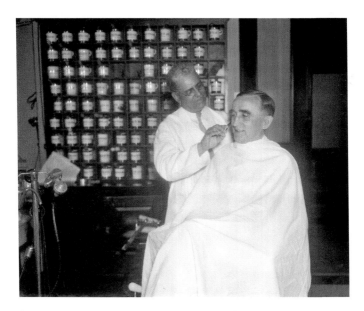

Senator Joseph Mahoney receiving a shave before taking the Senate floor, 1937. *Library of Congress.*

tired of that and entered Georgetown Law School, from which he graduated in 1920, which would indicate that he served as an editor in Cheyenne for only a year at most. This would make sense, as he was also employed as John B. Kendrick's secretary during this time frame, and he was not doubt working on his law degree concurrently. He replaced Kendrick upon his death. With a brief break, he would be a U.S. senator until leaving office in 1960.

1944 The 115th Cavalry, Wyoming National Guard, is broken into three separate units. After having been federalized in 1940, the unit was used early in the war to patrol the Pacific Coast. It was then heavily cadred out as experienced men were sent to other units. Ultimately, the late war unit, of which a majority of the men were no longer Wyoming National Guardsmen, saw only the headquarters and headquarters troop, 115th Cavalry Group, sent overseas into action.

1948 The hospital in Rock Springs is transferred from state ownership to Sweetwater County's ownership.

January 2

1949 This date marks the beginning of the great blizzard that struck the Northern Plains this year. In Wyoming, the storm started on this date and lasted until February 20. Snowfall in some areas measured up to thirty inches. The storm halted inter-town transport of all kinds within the state for twenty-four hours. Seventeen people died as a result of the storm, and 55,000 head of cattle and 105,000 head of sheep were lost.

January 3

1943 The prisoner of war camp is approved for Douglas.

There were POW camps all over the western United States during World War II. Locally, at least, Douglas, Wyoming; Scotsbluff, Nebraska; and Fort Robinson, Nebraska, had POW camps. There were probably additional locations nearby that have left no trace. Locating POW camps in

The sole remaining structure of the once-sprawling POW camp in Douglas, Wyoming. Next to nothing remains of the camp today. This is typical for these wartime installations. They were not really well built to start with, and there was no thought at all given to preserving them for any reasons. Today, the Douglas POW camp is down to one building, depicted here. This building was used as an officers' club for American officers stationed at the POW camp, and it contains some murals painted by Italian POWs. The "IOOF" on the building represents its postwar use as an Oddfellows lodge. *Photograph by the author.*

the West made sense. The vast terrain made escape nearly impossible. Some attempts were made, of course, and a few were successful, but not too many. Douglas, in fact, had one such escape by German prisoners, who were recaptured after a few days. At the time of their recapture, they asked what state they were in and were surprised to learn that they hadn't even made it out of Converse County.

January 4

1897 Big Horn County is organized.

1915 John B. Kendrick takes office as governor.

1943 Lester Hunt takes office as governor.

January 5

1883 Cheyenne is lighted by electric lights.

1904 A stage play based on Owen Wister's novel *The Virginian* opens on Broadway in New York. This is remarkable in that the novel had been written only two years earlier, showing the enormous popularity of what is, to some degree, the archetype of the western novel. The book, and hence the play, is set entirely in Wyoming and is loosely based on the strife in Wyoming's cattle industry of the 1880s and 1890s.

1925 Nellie T. Ross succeeds her late husband as governor of Wyoming, becoming the first female governor in U.S. history. She won her first election easily but was narrowly defeated in the 1926 election, during which her refusal to campaign for herself and her support of Prohibition hurt her. She later went on to be superintendent of mints in the Franklin Roosevelt administration. She's an interesting political figure in that not only was she the first female governor in the United States, but also her career was accidental. Never well off financially, keeping her career going was a necessity from the very onset, as her husband had borrowed money from his life insurance policy in order to run for governor. She lived to be 101 years old.

1959 John J. Hickey takes office as governor.

1975 Ed Herschler begins his twelve years as governor.

1987 Mike Sullivan takes office as governor. Sullivan would later serve as ambassador to Ireland under President Clinton.

January 6

1892 Gillette is incorporated.

1943 Governor Lester Hunt urges gifts of books to servicemen.

January 7

1865 Cheyenne, Arapaho and Sioux warriors attack Julesburg, Colorado, in retaliation for the Sand Creek Massacre by Colorado and New Mexico militia on November 29, 1864. Various bands of these tribes would continue north into Wyoming during this winter. Today, their general path is marked as the Sand Creek Massacre Trail on state and interstate highways in Wyoming and Colorado.

A highway sign marking the Sand Creek Massacre Trail. *Photograph by Marcus Holscher.*

1994 Natrona County High School is added to the National Register of Historic Places.

Natrona County High School is a major Natrona County landmark and serves with Kelly Walsh, Roosevelt and Midwest as one of the four high schools in the county, an unusual number for a Wyoming county. The school was built in 1923 and is presently undergoing massive renovation. When built, this nice yard didn't exist; rather, a public street ran right past the front. Well-known graduates include Dick Cheney, former vice president of the United States; Dean Conger, *National Geographic* photographer; Olympian Lance Deal; professional baseball player Mike Lansing; actor Geoffrey Lower (a member of my graduating class); and NBC news correspondent Pete Williams, who also was the photographer at my parents' wedding. *Photograph by the author.*

1997 Current Wyoming senator Mike Enzi takes office.

January 8

1884 The territorial legislature convenes in Cheyenne.

1933 Seven hundred rabbits are killed in a rabbit hunt at Thermopolis. This Depression-era event would prove to be very common in Wyoming in these years.

1943 Wyoming announces its first winter antelope season. The animal is emblematic of Wyoming today and is so numerous that it constitutes traffic hazards within the city limits of Casper.

January 9

1867 Laramie County is created by the Dakota territorial legislature.

1875 The officers' quarters at Fort D.A. Russell are destroyed by fire.

1887 A blizzard hits Wyoming and Montana with record snowfall and record cold, making this one of the worst days of the worst winters on record. The winter remains a killer legend for its horrific impact on the early Open Range cattle industry, which it nearly terminated.

January 10

1870 Standard Oil is incorporated. Standard would be a significant oil refiner in Wyoming, including having a massive refinery in the twentieth century bordering Casper.

1891 The legislature approves a Great Seal, but the matter results in an embarrassing controversy as one legislator switches his design for the one actually approved. Neither the original approved seal nor the bogus seal was used during the controversy, and a later seal was approved, which ended the matter.

1917 William F. Cody dies.

William F. Cody in 1911. The legendary showman is heavily associated with Wyoming and was the founder of the town in northern Wyoming named after him. A nearby irrigation project also commemorates him in the name of the dam, the Buffalo Bill Dam. He is not buried in Wyoming, however, which has been a bone of contention between Colorado, where he is buried, and Wyoming. His grave in Colorado has been reinforced to prevent Wyoming from taking it, although there was never any threat that Wyoming would. *Library of Congress.*

1922 The Laramie County sheriff conducts a series of raids on stills.

January 11

1868 A Vigilance Committee is formed in Cheyenne.

1888 The great blizzard of 1888 comes into Wyoming in full force. The storm is regarded as the worst in Wyoming's history, killing a fair number of people and hundreds, if not thousands, of cattle. The winter itself was the worst in Wyoming's history and was devastating on the livestock industry of the Northern Plains, putting many ranches permanently out of business and causing operational changes among those that survived. Oddly enough, the East Coast of the United States also had a huge blizzard in 1888.

1929 The Cambria casino dance hall opens in Niobrara County.

1970 Fire destroys two downtown blocks in Cheyenne.

January 12

1886 An explosion in the Almy coal mine kills thirteen miners.

1963 Rock Springs hits its record low of negative thirty-seven degrees Fahrenheit.

January 13

1877 Corporal Charles A. Bessey, Company A, Third U.S. Cavalry, wins the Congressional Medal of Honor for an action near Elkhorn Creek, Wyoming, on January 13, 1877: "While scouting with 4 men and attacked in ambush by 14 hostile Indians, held his ground, 2 of his men being wounded, and kept up the fight until himself wounded in the side, and then went to the assistance of his wounded comrades." Elkhorn is a common name for creeks in Wyoming, so exactly where this occurred I do not know.

1888 The post office at Fort D.A. Russell is reestablished.

1890 Union Pacific carpenters go on strike in Cheyenne.

1899 U.S. senator F.E. Warren introduces a bill for the erection of a U.S. Army post near Sheridan, Wyoming.

January 14

1868 A Vigilance Committee in Cheyenne threatens three suspected thieves.

1920 The first fatal air accident to occur near Casper occurs, taking the life of pilot Bert Cole and passenger Maud Toomey. Ms. Toomey is also the first female air fatality in Wyoming. The very early airport in use at this time was located where the town of Evansville now sits, and a memorial to Ms. Toomey, who was a schoolteacher, is located in Evansville.

1981 Peggy Simpson Curry is named state poet laureate. She was the first person to be so designated. She was born in Scotland in 1911 and immigrated as a child to Walden, Colorado, where her parents worked on a ranch. She moved to Wyoming to attend the University of Wyoming, where she majored in journalism and met her husband. She later taught at Casper College.

While she was memorialized as a poet, she wrote widely in other genres, having published novels and children's literature as well. She died in 1987.

She gave a reading, I recall, in my grade school in the 1960s and, with her booming and high-pitched voice, pretty much scared me to death.

January 15

1883 Cheyenne puts in electric streetlights.

1890 The eleventh and final territorial legislature is convened.

1890 The Wyoming Supreme Court, in the first of what has come to be an ongoing series of decisions, finds Wyoming's system for funding public schools unconstitutional. Debate on this topic kept up right through the 1990s.

Wyoming Supreme Court. The current courthouse was built in the 1930s and sits less than one block away from the State Capitol Building. *Photograph by the author.*

1991 The 1022nd Medical Company, Wyoming Army National Guard, deploys to Saudi Arabia.

January 16

1882 HR 3174 is introduced by Congressman Post, of Wyoming, to construct a military road from Fort Washakie to Yellowstone Park. Adversely reported later by the Military Affairs Committee.

1910 Work is completed on the Buffalo Bill Dam.

1920 Prohibition begins as the Eighteenth Amendment to the U.S. Constitution takes effect. Wyoming's politicians were surprisingly supportive of Prohibition, even though the population began evading it from the onset of the Volstead Act.

1924 First aircraft lands at Pinedale.

1943 A B-17 bomber does a ground loop in high winds at the Casper Air Base. Wind was a contributing cause.

A B-17 in the hangar at Casper Air Base, 1943. The Casper Air Base was a major training installation in Natrona County during World War II. *Courtesy of Wyoming State Archives, Department of State Parks and Cultural Resources.*

1953 Wyoming's long National Guard association with cavalry ends when the 115th Cavalry becomes the 349th Armored Field Artillery. The 115th had not been activated during the ongoing Korean War.

January 17

1930 Kendall, Wyoming, hits negative fifty-two degrees Fahrenheit.

1955 The 141st Medium Tank Battalion, Wyoming Army National Guard, which had been mobilized due to the Korean War but was not sent overseas, is deactivated.

January 18

1890 The editor of the Rawlins newspaper says unmarried men should be taxed $2.50.

1890 The U.S. Senate Committee on Territories recommends a bill to the Senate to make Wyoming a state.

January 19

1845 Joseph M. Carey is born in Milton, Delaware. He was an 1864 graduate of the University of Pennsylvania College of Law and was admitted to the Pennsylvania bar in 1867. He moved to Wyoming in 1869 and became the first United States attorney for Wyoming. He soon served on the Territorial Supreme Court before becoming a Natrona County rancher in 1876. He entered politics thereafter and became a U.S. congressman, senator and governor of Wyoming.

Joseph M. Carey and family while he was serving as governor of Wyoming. *Bain News Service Photograph, Library of Congress.*

1896 Butch Cassidy (Robert LeRoy Parker) is released from the state penitentiary after serving a term for horse theft.

Robert LeRoy Parker, aka Butch Cassidy, while a prisoner at the Wyoming State Penitentiary, which was at that time in Laramie. The old penitentiary was closed in favor of a new one in Rawlins some years later, which in turn has been replaced by a more modern facility, also in Rawlins. The old territorial prison, where Cassidy served time, was for a time used by the University of Wyoming as a sheep barn but now is a museum. *Courtesy of Wyoming State Archives, Department of State Parks and Cultural Resources.*

1911 Park County is organized.

1912 The Right Reverend Patrick A. McGovern is named the bishop of the Catholic Diocese of Cheyenne.

1938 The first concrete is poured on the construction of Seminoe Dam, a major dam on the North Platte in central Wyoming. The North Platte is, by some measures, the "most controlled river in the world."

January 20

1913 A riot breaks out in the Wyoming legislature.

1917 Legislature submits an act for a constitutional amendment that would allow people to vote on Prohibition.

January 21

1893 A criminal case against the Johnson County invaders is dismissed in Cheyenne, Wyoming. The trial had been held in Laramie County (Cheyenne), which was a jurisdiction favorable to them, rather than in Johnson County, which was not, but Johnson County lacked adequate facilities to hold all the prisoners.

Johnson County invaders. *Courtesy of Wyoming State Archives, Department of State Parks and Cultural Resources.*

1949 Legislature passes a bill prohibiting drunk flying. That this would be a bad idea seems self-evident.

January 22

1877 Sergeant William B. Lewis, Company B, Third U.S. Cavalry, is engaged in an action at Bluff Station, Wyoming, for which he won the Congressional Medal of Honor. Sergeant Lewis lived until 1901 and is buried in New Rochelle, New York.

1885 Crook County is organized. The county is named for General Crook, a serving and significant general in the Indian Wars.

1921 The legislature legalizes prizefighting. Prizefighting was actually illegal in most U.S. states in the late nineteenth and early twentieth centuries.

1949 The Reverend John Roberts, a significant Episcopal churchman on the Wind River Reservation, dies.

January 23

1899 Residents of Kemmerer vote to incorporate.

1901 Legislature meets in a joint session to pick a senator. Francis E. Warren is chosen to fill the office.

January 24

1873 Congress approves funds to rebuild the territorial penitentiary in Laramie. This facility would serve for many years until a new penitentiary was built in Rawlins. It later became the University of Wyoming's sheep barn and is now a museum.

1878 General Cook states that there is no military need to keep troops at Fort Fred Steele or Fort Sanders, two posts in southern Wyoming on the Union Pacific.

1945 The legislature rejects a junior college plan. Much of Wyoming's higher education story in the second half of the twentieth century was centered on tension between those favoring the expansion of community colleges, which ultimately became a fact, and those favoring keeping those resources in the University of Wyoming. By the late twentieth century, those tensions had been resolved to the point where the university had a presence on many of the community college campuses.

January 25

1897 Shoshone chief Washakie is baptized by Episcopal priest John Roberts.

Chief Washakie in 1886. Chief Washakie lived to be about one hundred years old and is one of the most significant personages in Wyoming's history. *Courtesy of Wyoming State Archives, Department of State Parks and Cultural Resources.*

1915 The modern Wyoming Bar Association is formed. Wyoming has a self-governing bar, and the Bar Association serves a semi-governmental function in that capacity. At the time of its inception, it had ninety-five members.

1967 Jade is adopted as the state gemstone.

January 26

1905 John J. Pershing marries Frances Warren in Cheyenne, Wyoming. Pershing was, therefore, Senator Warren's son-in-law. He would, of course, go on to command U.S. troops in the Punitive Expedition into Mexico and then all U.S. forces in Europe during World War I. Frances Warren would die in a tragic fire at the Presidio in California just prior to the Punitive Expedition, while her husband was away on border service.

1914 The Hotel LeBonte opens in Douglas. The building is still there.

1932 An earthquake occurs in Yellowstone that is felt regionally.

January 27

1878 General Philip H. Sheridan recommends the removal of the garrison at Camp Stambaugh.

1880 Thomas Edison receives a patent for his electric incandescent lamp. The concept for the invention first came to Edison while he was in Wyoming on a trip to view an eclipse.

1920 Wyoming ratifies the Nineteenth Amendment to the U.S. Constitution.

1943 Contact is reestablished with Jackson after the town had been isolated due to a snowstorm. The period of no contact was six days.

This was not really an unusual event at the time. Prior to advancements in 4x4 vehicles, brought about due to World War II, it was nearly impossible to remove significant amounts of snow from mountain passes, and towns located in mountain valleys were routinely cut off from contact with the outside for days and even weeks. This was particularly true for Jackson. Indeed, this was so much the case that a book written in the 1950s by a screenwriter who lived in the town off and on during the '40s and '50s maintained that the "Cocktail Hour in Jackson Hole" was the entire winter, as the town was completely cut off from the outside during that time and engaged in one huge party all winter long. No doubt that was an exaggeration, but there was some truth to the statement.

Less romantic, the irony of the situation is that up until the 1970s, Jackson was not regarded as a particularly desirable place to live. This was very much the case prior to 1950. At that time, agriculture, together with government agencies, formed the economic base of the town, but even the homesteads that had been filed there were very late ones and were not the most enviable to have, as the ranches in the valley had to combat the weather and were so extremely isolated. It is only the modern 4x4 snow plow that has made Jackson the winter vacation spot it is and, by extension, the home of many wealthy people.

January 28

1912 Paul Jackson Pollock is born in Cody, Wyoming. He became famous for art that featured paint splatters and remains a controversial art figure. He mostly grew up outside the state, however, and his artwork could probably be searched for extensively in Wyoming without being found very easily.

Pollock struggled with alcoholism his entire short life and died in a car wreck when he was driving under the influence.

1949 Eighteen Wyoming counties ask for emergency relief to clear snow following blizzards.

January 29

1870 Sweetwater County is organized as Carter County, with South Pass City as the county seat.

1958 Killer Charles Starkweather is apprehended by sheriff's officers in Wyoming.

January 30

1912 A coal mine explosion in Kemmerer kills five.

January 31

1876 The U.S. government issues an order that all Indians on the Northern Plains must return to their agencies.

1917 The Indian Paintbrush is chosen as the state flower.

1917 A design for Wyoming's flag is chosen. The flag was designed by Mrs. A.C. Keyes of Casper, formerly Miss Verna Keays of Buffalo.

Flags at half mast at Casper College in memory of Chief Warrant Officer Andrew McAdams, twenty-seven, killed when an MC-12 reconnaissance aircraft crashed in Afghanistan during a nighttime mission on January 14, 2014. *Photograph by the author.*

1938 James Watt, secretary of the interior in the Reagan administration, is born in Lusk. Watt was a very controversial secretary, an office that rarely generates controversy outside the West itself.

FEBRUARY IN WYOMING

In much of the country, February is the month in which people ponder Groundhog Day and what it means for the prolongation of winter. In a normal winter in Wyoming, however, no such contemplation need be made. February is a deep winter month in the state. Average temperatures range from eighteen to forty-one degrees Fahrenheit. Skiing, snowshoeing and snowmobiling are still in swing, but the end of the winter sports is in sight. The end of "feeding" of range cattle, however, is not.

February 1

1876 The secretary of the interior reports that Sitting Bull's band has not reported to the reservation, and the matter is turned over to the Department of the Army.

1943 A bill requiring premarital tests for women is signed by Governor Hunt. Such a bill would be regarded as an unconscionable sexist act today, but in the medical context of the time, it was a rational attempt at controlling the spread of certain diseases.

2007 Montana files suit against Wyoming and North Dakota in the Supreme Court, which has original jurisdiction over suits between states, concerning water appropriations from the Tongue and Powder Rivers. Oral arguments were heard on January 10, 2011, in the cause. The court issued its decision on May 2, 2011.

February 2—Groundhog Day

1943 The Wyoming Supreme Court determines that it is not possible to contract common-law marriages in Wyoming.

1958 Warren Air Force Base becomes part of the Strategic Air Command, in keeping with its role as a missile base.

February 3

1876 The first stage running from Cheyenne to the Black Hills leaves Cheyenne.

1919 The legislature passes a joint resolution in favor of national women's suffrage.

February 4

1889 Harry Lonabaugh, more commonly known as the Sundance Kid, is pardoned by Wyoming territorial governor Moonlight. Lonabaugh was serving time in the Crook County Jail in Sundance, Wyoming, for having stolen a horse, saddle and firearm.

Lonabaugh would work as a cowboy in Alberta after his release from the Crook County Jail. He returned to Wyoming sometime around 1896 and formed the Hole in the Wall Gang with Robert Leroy Parker,

Harry Lonabaugh and Etta Place. *Library of Congress.*

better known as Butch Cassidy. The gang had wide-ranging criminal activity, conducting robberies as far south as Utah. In 1901, Lonabaugh and Parker, together with Etta Place, left for South America, where Parker and Lonabaugh would ultimately be killed in Bolivia in 1908 in a gun battle with a small party of Bolivian cavalrymen and police.

Place, pictured on the previous page, was the paramour or perhaps wife of Lonabaugh, taking his mother's maiden name for her last name, although she also used Lonabaugh. She has the distinction of being the first woman in Argentina to have acquired land under that country's 1884 homestead act, at which time Lonabaugh also acquired a sizable land grant. Lonabaugh and Place oddly returned to the United States at least twice in the 1901 to 1904 time frame, even though the Pinkerton Agency was hunting for them. They abandoned their ranches in Argentina when the Pinkerton agency tracked them there and secured Argentine arrest warrants for them. Place returned to the United States a third time with Lonabaugh in 1905 and remained when he returned to South America. Her ultimate fate is unknown.

1899 The Wyoming battalion is attached to the Second Brigade, First Division, for service in the Philippines.

1903 Willis Van Devanter, at that time teaching at George Washington Law School, is nominated by Theodore Roosevelt to the position of justice of the Eighth Circuit Court of Appeals.

1905 Construction starts on Pathfinder Dam between Casper and Rawlins.

Recent construction raised the height of the dam to take into account a century of silting. Pathfinder is a major central Wyoming recreational site, attracting fishermen from all over the state and neighboring states in both winter and summer. Winter fishing is, of course, ice fishing, as the lake is six thousand feet in elevation.

A photomechanical Bureau of Reclamation print of Pathfinder Dam under construction. This view couldn't be observed today, as it looks at the dam from the flooded side. *Library of Congress.*

1955 Bear River Compact between Wyoming and Utah is approved.

February 5

1876 John Henry "Doc" Holliday moves to Cheyenne, where he worked at the Bella Union as a gaming dealer.

1924 Joseph M. Carey, governor from 1911 to 1915 and member of the Republican and Progressive Parties, dies in Cheyenne.

1927 The meadowlark is designated the state bird.

1943 The legislature passes a bill denying American citizens interned at Heart Mountain Relocation Camp the right to vote. While the legislation seems shocking in retrospect, although probably not as shocking as internment, there was somewhat of a basis for the concept in that the Heart Mountain internees were involuntarily residents of Wyoming and therefore not residents. In hindsight, if attempted today, it seems clear that this result would no longer be regarded as legitimate, but internment would also no longer be regarded as legitimate.

February 6

1899 The Spanish-American War ends. The Spanish-American War was the first American war that the state of Wyoming participated in. Even during the Indian Wars, the state itself, which of course became a state only after the main part of the fighting was over, had a very small role. The Spanish-American War, however, was different.

Almost completely forgotten now, the war was controversial and not well received in some parts of the East. In the West, however, it was enthusiastically approached. Wyoming was one of the locations where volunteer cavalry regiments were formed, although

A photograph of the distinctive unit insignia of the Wyoming Army National Guard on the standard-issue army black beret. *Photograph by the author.*

Wyoming's unit, the Third U.S. Volunteer Cavalry, never made it overseas (of the volunteer cavalry regiments, only the First U.S. Volunteer Cavalry did). Tragically, Wyoming's contribution did sustain serious casualties, including deaths in a train accident as the men were being sent to Florida prior to the invasion of Cuba. The war is memorialized today in a memorial on the capitol grounds.

The Third U.S. Volunteer Cavalry is still recalled today in the general form of the Wyoming Army National Guard unit patch, which features a roughrider. Not all Wyoming Army National Guard units wear the patch, as they once did, but some still do.

February 7

1872 Snow continues to prevent trains from traveling from Cheyenne to Denver, as it had since December 20.

1888 The territorial legislature passes a petition to Congress to organize as a state.

1902 Casper's town council legalizes gambling in Casper. The legislature would later regulate, and largely outlaw, gambling statewide, but gambling in Casper remained an open activity into the 1950s. At least one bar in the town ran a gambling board for betting on sports.

February 8

1893 Confusion over the design for the state seal leads the legislature to adopt more specific language, providing:

A pedestal showing on the front thereof an eagle resting upon a shield, said shield to have engraving thereon a star and the figures "44," being the number of Wyoming in the order of admission to statehood. Standing upon the pedestal shall be the draped figure of a woman, modeled after the statue of the "Victory" in the Louvre, from whose wrists shall hang links of a broken chain, and holding in her right hand a staff, from the top of which shall float a banner with the words "Equal Rights" thereon, all suggesting the political position of woman in this state. On either side of the pedestal, and standing at the base thereof, shall be male figures typifying the livestock and mining industries of Wyoming. Behind the pedestal, and in the background, shall be two pillars, each supporting a lighted lamp, signifying the light of knowledge. Around each pillar shall be a scroll with the following words thereon: On the right of the central figure the words "Live Stock" and "Grain." and on the left the words "Mines" and "Oil." At the base of the pedestal, and in front shall appear the figures "1869–1890," the former date signifying the organization of the Territory of Wyoming, and the latter the date of its admission to statehood. A facsimile of the above described seal is here represented and is made a part of this act.

The original approved design was substituted by the legislator who carried the seal design to Governor Barber for his own, which had not won approval. That design featured a woman bereft of clothing in the design. When the governor learned of the switch, he commissioned a drawing of the correct seal, but by that time, the matter had become such a controversy that it was kept secret and not used. Ultimately, money printed with Wyoming's seal in this period—and there were notes printed with the seals of every state at this time—used a modified territorial seal.

1919 Edwin Keith Thomson is born in Newcastle. Thomson had risen spectacularly young, graduating from the University of Wyoming College of Law in 1941 at which time he was only twenty-two years old. He entered the service thereafter and became the youngest battalion commander in the U.S. Army during World War II, reaching that position at age twenty-four. He was still in his twenties when discharged as a lieutenant colonel in 1946. He became the congressman from Wyoming in 1955. He was elected to the Senate in 1960 but died of a heart attack at age forty-one before assuming office. His widow, Thyra Thomson, served as Wyoming's secretary of state for twenty-four years.

1938 Alcova Dam is completed.

1941 Willis Van Devanter dies. Van Devanter achieved a lasting position in U.S. history due to his elevation to the United States Supreme Court, the only member of the Wyoming State Bar to achieve that honor. He had retired in 1937, after Congress granted full pay to justices over seventy years of age who retired. He stayed in Washington, D.C., where he is buried.

Willis Van Devanter. Van Devanter is mostly remembered in the United States for his role as a long-serving conservative Supreme Court justice, one of the ones who aggravated Franklin D. Roosevelt. In Wyoming, he is more controversially recalled as one of the cattlemen's attorneys during the Johnson County invaders' trial and for representing the Wyoming Stock Growers Association during its controversial era. *Library of Congress.*

1943 A B-25 lands on a highway near Douglas due to low fuel.

February 9

1893 Wyoming is divided into four judicial districts by the legislature. The number has been expanded to the current day, there now being nine judicial districts, several of which encompass a single county.

1916 Bill Carlisle robs passengers on the Union Pacific Portland Rose.

1933 The coldest recorded temperature in the state is set at the Riverside Ranger Station in Yellowstone National Park at negative sixty-six degrees Fahrenheit. On the same day, a series of cold records was established in the region, such as negative sixty-three degrees at Moran.

February 10

1875 John M. Thayer begins his second term as territorial governor.

1876 General Terry is ordered to take action against the Sioux and Cheyenne who remain off their reservations. This order essentially marks the beginning of the campaigns of 1876 and 1877, which would see so much action in Wyoming and Montana.

1883 Long-serving Episcopal missionary Reverend John Roberts arrives at Fort Washakie.

1890 Eleven million acres ceded by the Sioux are opened for entry.

1904 The United States secretary of the interior sets aside $2,250,000 for the initial construction of the Shoshone Project, including a dam, which was one of the first federal reclamation projects in the nation and the largest federal project in Wyoming. The entire water project would take years to complete.

1980 Floyd Taliaferro Alderson dies in Sheridan. Alderson had been an early movie star, acting at first under the name Wally Wales and later as Hal Taliaferro. He was born in Sheridan in 1895 and grew up on the family ranch in Montana, where he returned after his acting career concluded.

February 11

1805 Sacajawea gives birth to her first child, Jean Baptiste Charbonneau, at Fort Mandan, in what is now North Dakota.

Sacajawea was a Shoshone who was a member of the Lemhi band. She was likely born in Idaho, although the Shoshone ranged throughout Wyoming and Idaho and the Lemhi ranged in northern Idaho and Wyoming. She was kidnapped in a tribal raid by the Hidatsa when she was about twelve, which gives rise to Hidatsa claims that she was a Hidatsa, although the claim is not correct. She lived with them for only about a year before being purchased by Touissant Charbonneau, a French Canadian trapper. Charbonneau was a polygamist, as he had earlier also married another young Indian girl, Otter Woman. Sacajawea was still in her teens when she gave birth to her son, Jean Baptiste.

It has been claimed that Jean Baptiste lived until 1885 and is buried, along with Sacajawea, on the Wind River Reservation, a claim that is advanced by some Shoshones. The evidence for this, however, is weak on both accounts, although a major feature of the Fort Washakie cemetery is a tombstone marking what purports to be her grave, that being a minor tourist attraction in the region. The better evidence is that neither died in Wyoming and that Jean Baptiste far outlived his mother but died in 1866 due to a sudden illness brought about by an accidental plunge into icy water in Oregon. Sacajawea is believed to have died in 1812, according to the most reliable accounts, of a nameless sickness. She would have been only about twenty-five years old at the time and a mother of two living children.

1911 Governor Carey signs the Direct Primary Law, which was part of a general movement toward such primaries throughout the United States.

February 12

1971 James Cash Penney dies in New York City. Penney, in partnership with Guy Johnson and Thomas Callahan, opened his first store in Kemmerer in 1902. He had been working for Johnson and Callahan in Golden Rule stores in Utah, and they had been impressed with him as an employee. Penney bought them out in 1917, and the franchise expanded rapidly thereafter. The company did have its ups and downs, and Penney himself had to fund the company by borrowing on his life insurance to keep it running during the Great Depression.

February 13

1865 First Lieutenant Henry C. Bretney assumes command of Company G, Eleventh Ohio Cavalry, stationed at Platte Bridge Station, when its commander, Captain Levi M. Rinehart, is accidentally killed by a drunken trooper during a skirmish with Indians.

1911 Campbell County is created.

1917 The Wyoming legislature appropriates $750 to move Jim Baker's cabin from Carbon County to Cheyenne. Baker was a frontiersman who came west working for the American Fur Company. He was later chief scout for General Harney out of Fort Laramie. In 1859, he homesteaded at a location that is now in Denver, Colorado. He held a commission in the Colorado State Militia during the Civil War. He relocated to a site near Savery, Wyoming, in 1873 and homesteaded there. He continued to ranch in that location until his death in 1898, although he did serve the U.S. Army as a scout occasionally in the 1870s.

Today, the cabin is located once again in Savery. It is an unusual structure, as it was built partially as a blockhouse in case of attack.

It's interesting to note that a concern for preserving the early history of the state became quite pronounced during this period.

1942 All Japanese nationals employed by the Union Pacific Railroad are dismissed.

February 14 – St. Valentine's Day

1870 The Sweetwater County Board of Commissioners, in a vote of two to one, approves Esther Hobart Morris's application for justice of the peace. This made her the first female justice of the peace in the United States. She served for just about nine months. She served the full length of her term but could not secure a renomination from either political party in Sweetwater County. Of the cases she presided over that were appealed, not one was reversed. She lived until 1902 and is buried in Cheyenne.

1911 Niobrara County is created.

1971 A campaign is commenced to save the Ivinson Mansion in Laramie. It is now the Laramie Plains Museum. The substantial building had been constructed by the Ivinson family, early significant figures in Laramie, and belonged to the Episcopal Diocese of Wyoming at the time, which was considering selling it due to the costs involved in keeping it. The Ivinsons, immigrants from the Virgin Islands, were originally British citizens and were members of the Episcopal Church. The impressive structure is familiar to anyone who has spent any time in Laramie.

February 15

1812 The Astorians reach the mouth of the Columbia River. They traveled overland with one horse for every two men. Their route had taken them through Wyoming and over South Pass.

1869 Laramie's first school opens.

1909 Park County is formed.

1921 Teton County is formed.

1921 Sublette County is formed.

2006 Cheyenne's Union Pacific Depot is declared a National Historic Landmark.

Union Pacific Depot in Cheyenne, which the UP had at one time declared to be the most beautiful depot in the world. *Photograph by the author.*

February 16

1890 Robert C. Morris suggests the "Equality State" as a state motto. Morris was the son of Esther Hobart Morris, and she lived with him in his house in Cheyenne in her later years. He was a legislator in the early twentieth century and served as the clerk of the Wyoming Supreme Court.

February 17

1870 Esther Hobart Morris is officially appointed justice of the peace. As noted, she was approved for this position several days prior.

A statue of Esther Hobart Morris located at the capitol in Cheyenne. Period photos of Justice Morris show her to be a less attractive and sterner-looking person, perhaps because they were all taken late in her rather hard life. *Photograph by the author.*

1933 The Blaine Act ends Prohibition at the federal level. Contrary to popular imagination, it didn't necessarily end it everywhere in the United States, as many states, including Wyoming, had separate and additional Prohibition statutes. Wyoming chose to roll back Prohibition in stages, with a commission made up of significant churchmen, statesmen and politicians empaneled for that purpose. The

The bar at the Virginian in Medicine Bow. This bar is still there next to the restaurant. *Courtesy of Wyoming State Archives, Department of State Parks and Cultural Resources.*

goal was to prohibit the return of unregulated saloons. The process created a somewhat unique state-controlled system in which all alcohol flows through the state liquor warehouse and is distributed by the state.

Repeal would see a vast number of Wyoming bars reestablished, however.

February 18

1862 U.S. Congress approves an act entitled "An Act to Grant Lands to Dakota, Montana, Arizona, Idaho and Wyoming for University Purposes." This crated "land grant" universities. The act was broad enough that it ultimately even included a few high schools, with Natrona County High School in Casper being one such example. The University of Wyoming was a land grant college.

1933 Governor Miller signs an act repealing enforcement of Prohibition by Wyoming. The repeal was actually only partial at first, and it took a period of many months before there was a complete repeal.

1987 The cutthroat trout is declared to be the state fish.

February 19

1887 The final run of the Black Hills stage leaves Cheyenne.

1901 A bill prohibiting gambling is signed into law.

1917 The State Highway Commission is created by the signature of the governor of an act approving it.

1942 Franklin D. Roosevelt signs Executive Order 9066, authorizing the removal of any or all people from military areas "as deemed necessary or desirable." This would lead to internment camps, including Heart Mountain near Cody.

February 20

1911 Governor Carey signs a bill carving Lincoln County out of Uinta County.

1919 The legislature appropriates $2,500 for placing markers along the Oregon Trail.

1923 The legislature experiences a fifty-six-hour "day" in a questionable legislature trick designed to keep the clock from winding up on the session. This trick has been repeated since then, but this one was the longest on record.

1949 The last day of the Blizzard of 1949, which was actually a series of blizzards that occurred in rapid succession.

Left: A rotary plow during the Blizzard of 1949. *Courtesy of Wyoming State Archives, Department of State Parks and Cultural Resources.*

Opposite: A snowdrift by Lusk, 1949. *Courtesy of Wyoming State Archives, Department of State Parks and Cultural Resources.*

February 21

1900 A military funeral is held for Chief Washakie.

1903 Wyoming establishes a gift and estate tax. Wyoming still has such a tax, but it applies only at very substantial income levels.

1925 The legislature passes a $0.02.5 gasoline tax. While this sounds quite small, in terms of the era, it was actually a fairly significant tax. Contrary to the common assumption, in real terms, gasoline of the era was quite expensive, and automobiles, which were already common, were very expensive to purchase and own.

February 22

1897 President Cleveland issues a proclamation establishing the Big Horn National Forest.

1899 The First Nebraska U.S. Volunteer Infantry and the Wyoming Battalion, volunteers, engage Philippine insurgents near Deposito. The action commenced at 0615 when the Wyoming Battalion, which had deployed about two hours earlier, encountered Philippine insurgents and opened fire. The action was sharp, with results being generally inconclusive.

February 23

1941 Blizzard conditions stall traffic in the state. This was, of course, in the pre-4x4 days. Prior to World War II, 4x4 vehicles were almost unheard of and were limited to industrial vehicles. Almost every vehicle was a rear-wheel-drive 2x4.

1950 A special session of the legislature called to deal with the problem of grasshopper infestation concludes.

1969 Governor Hathaway signs into law a state severance tax bill. The bill had been extremely controversial, with there being strong arguments by the opposition that passing it would cause Wyoming's extractive industries to greatly reduce their activity. The arguments failed to stop the bill, and the severance tax did not greatly impact the extractive industries. Today, Wyoming is nearly entirely funded by severance taxes.

1985 The bison is adopted as the state mammal.

February 24

1897 Wyoming accepts a grant of one mile square of land from the Wind River Reservation for the hot springs at what is now Thermopolis.

1941 The 115th Cavalry Regiment, Wyoming National Guard, is inducted into federal service.

February 25

1858 Fort Thompson is abandoned. The post near the present location of Lander had been in existence only since October 1857.

1868 Cheyenne passes an ordinance against gambling and disorderly houses.

1920 Woodrow Wilson signs the Minerals Leasing Act of 1920. This act created the modern system of leasing federal oil, gas and coal interests, which previously had been subject to claim under the Mining Law of 1872.

The extent to which this revolutionized the oil, gas and coal industries in economic terms can hardly be overestimated. Prior to 1920, these fossil fuels could be exploited via a simple mining claim, and the land itself could be patented after the claim was "proved up." The 1920 act ended this practice concerning these resources. (The 1872 act continues on for other minerals, in a very modified form, to the present day.) The leasing system meant that the resources never left the public domain in

Early Wyoming oil production. *Library of Congress.*

absolute terms, and the payment of the lease was a huge economic boon to the state and federal government.

1925 House Joint Memorial No. 4 approves "Memorializing the Congress of the United States to Set Aside Old Fort Laramie and Old Fort Bridger and Independence Rock as Historic Reserves."

1961 The legislature approves the purchase of the grounds of Fort Fetterman.

Top: A flagpole on the parade ground at Fort Fetterman. Not much of the original post remains today, but the foundations of buildings can be seen. *Photograph by the author.*

Right: Buildings at Fort Fetterman. *Photograph by the author.*

February 26

1929 President Calvin Coolidge signs an executive order establishing the Grand Teton National Park in Wyoming.

1970 South Pass City is added to the National Register of Historic Places.

February 27

1915 Governor Kendrick approves a workers' compensation act establishing a state-maintained workers' compensation fund. While heavily litigated, occasionally amended and often castigated, the basic structure of the groundbreaking 1915 act remains today. Somewhat unique in the United States, the Wyoming act created a wholly state-administered workers' compensation system in which workmen surrendered their rights to bring certain workplace civil actions and employers gave up their common-law defenses so that certain suits that had traditionally been available for personal injury in the workplace were eliminated in favor of a system of insurance, modeled on that pioneered in Imperial Germany.

The system remains exclusively state administered and run today and is funded by levies on employers, making it one of the few, and perhaps the only, solely state-run system in the United States today. Most states use a system that incorporates privately purchased workers' compensation insurance.

February 28

1885 F.E. Warren is confirmed as territorial governor.

February 29 —
Only Occurs in Leap Years

1288 Scotland makes it legal for a woman to propose marriage. (See 1912 item for Wyoming.)

1912 The *Wyoming Tribune* publishes the names of eligible bachelors for the benefit of "matrimonially inclined women." Things like this were surprisingly common at the time, and the publication on this date is not accidental, as this particular day was associated with Sadie Hawkins–type events.

1929 Grand Teton National Park is established by Congress. This entry seems somewhat inconsistent with an earlier entry made just a few days ago, so this might be the effective date of the establishment of the park, which was smaller at that time as compared to the current park.

MARCH IN WYOMING

March, Garrison Keillor famously observed in regard to Minnesota, is the month that informs people who do not drink what hangovers are like. That is somewhat true of March in Wyoming.

March offers hints of a true spring but also reminds Wyomingites that more winter is yet to come. People claim, elsewhere, that March comes in like a lamb and goes out like a lion, but in Wyoming, it comes in like a cold lion and goes out like one too. March is a winter month in Wyoming but with teases of spring-like weather to come. Skiing on ski runs is coming to an end, and in the backcountry, skiing can become dangerous in this month due to the risk of avalanches. Stockmen begin to plan for calving season, which hasn't quite arrived.

March 1

1872 Congress authorizes the creation of Yellowstone National Park.

Yellowstone National Park poster. *Library of Congress.*

1876 The 1876 Powder River Expedition sets out from Fort Fetterman. By leaving in early March, they were committing themselves to a march in what was still winter weather.

1877 Jack McCall, Wild Bill Hickok's killer, is arrested. Following the killing, he'd gone to Laramie, where his bragging about the killing and his making up a story about the killing of a fictional brother to cover it led to his arrest and, ultimately, his trial.

1913 Governor Carey approves an act of the legislature that creates two additional judicial districts. Today, there are nine.

1944 Fremont County, Wyoming agriculture agents request two hundred POWs for farm labor.

1957 KTWO in Casper starts operations as Wyoming's second television station.

March 2

1861 Congress creates the Dakota and Nevada Territories out of the Nebraska and Utah Territories. Wyoming was part of the Dakota Territory at that time.

1868 General Grant issues an order to abandon Fort Reno, Fort Kearny and Fort C.F. Smith on the Bozeman Trail. The fort abandonments were byproducts of the end of Red Cloud's War, which is regarded as the only Plains Indian War won by the native combatants.

The closure of the posts was not instant. It was winter in Wyoming and Montana, and the actual closings occurred in the summer.

1890 Fort Laramie's status as an active U.S. Army post ends.

Remains of cement buildings at Fort Laramie. This fort is highly unusual in that its pre–Civil War era buildings included some made of cement. *Photograph by the author.*

March 3

1805 President Jefferson approves the act that creates the Territory of Louisiana, which included much of Wyoming.

1849 The Home Department, a predecessor of the Interior Department, is established by the federal government. The Interior Department has a major influence on Wyoming and its economy, with nearly half of Wyoming being owned by the United States government.

1863 Parts of Wyoming are included in Idaho Territory, which is created by Congress on this day.

1870 A court empanels six women for a six-member jury for the first time in history.

1876 A nighttime raid takes horses and cattle from Crook's Powder River Expedition. The cattle are recovered but are driven to Fort Fetterman.

1879 Congress establishes the United States Geological Survey.

1884 Buffalo is incorporated.

The well-preserved late nineteenth- or early twentieth-century main street of Buffalo, Wyoming. *Photograph by the author.*

March 4

1881 A mine explosion in Almy kills thirty-one miners.

1882 Evanston is reincorporated.

1884 The legislature passes a tax authorization for the purpose of constructing a university.

1886 Governor Warren authorizes the construction of a capitol building, as just approved by the legislature.

The Wyoming State Capitol Building. *Photograph by the author.*

1886 The University of Wyoming is chartered.

1931 Fort Laramie National Historic Site is established.

March 5

1766 France cedes Louisiana to Spain.

1876 Bill Hickok marries Agnes Thatcher in Cheyenne.

1876 A nighttime raid is attempted on Crook's command on the Powder River Expedition, but it is detected prior to the attack.

1884 Territorial governor Hale approves the act creating Fremont County.

1889 The first school in Casper opens, a subscription school started by Mrs. Adah E. Allen. Schools of this type were very common in this period and reflected the local communities' desire to have primary education but also reflected a lack of state funding or uniformity. Concerns about the lack of uniformity and a very strong desire for public education in the West caused the creation of the elective office of superintendent of public instruction. Wyomingites have recently seen a great deal of controversy regarding this particular office, which the legislature has recently deprived of most of its powers; they are now vested in an appointed officer.

March 6

1866 William F. Cody marries Louisa Frederici in St. Louis.

1884 Sheridan, Wyoming, is incorporated. Sheridan is named after Philip Sheridan, who was born on this day.

March 7

1871 First National Bank of Cheyenne is chartered.

1890 A congressman from Illinois announces his opposition to Wyoming statehood due to the suffrage provision in the proposed state's constitution.

1899 The Philippine insurrection starts at San Juan del Monte with an assault by Philippine troops. The first shot was fired by an Englishman serving in the Nebraska volunteers, followed by shots fired by Nebraska and Wyoming volunteers, and soon other troops from state volunteer units were engaged. The Philippine forces initially took some American positions, but by the end of the day, positions were retaken.

1944 It is announced that the Wyoming State Hospital at Rock Springs will be training nurses for the U.S. Army.

March 8

1941 National Guardsmen parade in Casper prior to deployment. Apparently, 160 men were in the parade, although I would have thought the 115th Cavalry would have been fully activated by this time.

1977 Martin's Cove is added to the National Register of Historic Places.

March 9

1820 Congress passes the Land Act, which prohibited the purchase of the public domain on credit, reduced the size of the minimum purchase to eighty acres and required a down payment of $100.00—a substantial amount—but reduced the per acreage price to $1.25. The act was designed to help stop speculation in public land and assist small purchasers.

1888 Natrona, Converse and Sheridan Counties are created by the territorial legislature. This overrode a veto by the territorial governor.

1904 A sheep raid near Laramie results in the destruction of sheep camps and the death of three hundred sheep. The early twentieth century in Wyoming was marked by a sheep war that went on for nearly a decade, during which time cattle interests resorted to violence in an effort to keep mostly nomadic sheep operations out of the state. Attacks on sheep camps became common during this period.

March 10

1804 A formal ceremony is held in St. Louis involving the transfer of Louisiana to Spain, back to France and then to the United States. The inclusion of Spain was due to a legal oddity regarding France's acquisition of Louisiana.

1848 The Treaty of Guadalupe Hidalgo ends the Mexican War.

1866 The U.S. Army's General Pope organizes the military Mountain District and orders the establishment of Fort Philip Kearny and Fort C.F. Smith to protect the Bozeman Trail.

1875 Union Pacific shareholders resolve to erect Ames Monument between Laramie and Cheyenne in honor of Oakes Ames and Oliver Ames Jr., two Union Pacific financiers.

1890 Members of the Albany County Council state that the light air of the county causes insanity.

March 11

1824 The War Department creates the Bureau of Indian Affairs.

1883 Alfred Packer is arrested near Fort Fetterman, Wyoming. Packer was wanted for murder and the following cannibalism of his fellows in the Colorado mountains while they were wintering over in a gold-seeking expedition in 1873–74. Packer denied the charges at first but ultimately confessed and was twice convicted. His 1883 arrest reflects his attempt to flee in 1874, after his first confession. He received a forty-year sentence for his crimes but was released in 1901 and thereafter went to work as a guard for the *Denver Post*.

A dining hall at the University of Colorado is mischievously named the Alfred G. Packer Memorial Grill and sports the motto: "Have a friend for lunch!" A menu item is the "El Canibal." The school features an "Alfred Packer Days" event.

Packer twice enlisted in the U.S. Army during the Civil War. He first served in the Sixteenth Infantry but was discharged after several months due to epilepsy. He later joined the Eighth Iowa Cavalry but was again discharged for the same reason.

1887 Calamity Jane is reported to be in town by a Cheyenne newspaper.

1888 Sheridan County is organized.

March 12

1886 The legislature appropriates $500 for Governor William Hale's funeral and a monument in his honor.

1888 Territorial governor Thomas Moonlight hires the legendary Elwood Mead as state engineer. Mead was the founder of Wyoming's water law, which he worked on from 1888 to 1899. He also worked on Colorado's water law during this period. In 1907, he was appointed chairman of the State Rivers and Water Supply Commission in Victoria, Australia. He returned to the United States in 1911 and became a professor of rural institutions at the University of California. He led the Bureau of Reclamation in the Coolidge administration. Lake Mead is named after him.

1890 Big Horn and Weston Counties are created.

March 13

1908 An American car reaches Evanston in a New York–to-Paris race. The early automobile era saw some spectacular races and efforts of this type. At the time, highways in the region were simply dirt roads.

1918 The Ohio Oil Company commences drilling a well that would become the first Lance Creek–area oil well. The field actually came about prior to the Mineral Leasing Act, so many of the oil claims were filed under the Mining Law of 1872 as "placer" claims. The area would boom enormously during World War II due to oil exploration but would drop off dramatically thereafter.

1974 Arab nations decide to end the oil embargo on the United States.

March 14

1850 A post office is established at Fort Laramie, the first in Wyoming.

March 15

1924 The wreck of the six-masted schooner *Wyoming* is located off Pollock Rip, Massachusetts. It went down with all eighteen hands.

1939 Deputy Park County sheriff D.M. Baker and Powell police marshal Charles Lewis are shot by Earl Durand, soon to be dubbed the "Tarzan of the Tetons," when they are attempting to arrest him at his parents' home. Durand had been in the county jail for poaching and had escaped after assaulting a jailor. This would commence his ten-day flight into the local mountains, which concluded in a failed attempt to rob the bank in Powell, during which he was killed.

1943 Franklin Roosevelt uses executive authority to proclaim 221,000 acres as the Jackson Hole National Monument, the predecessor to today's Grand Teton National Park.

March 16

1963 Workmen commence pouring cement for the Yellowtail Dam for the Big Horn Reservoir.

March 17 — St. Patrick's Day

The feast day falls on the anniversary of St. Patrick's death in Saul, Ireland, in the year 461 or 493.

St. Patrick is the patron saint of Ireland. Wyoming has a relatively large Irish community, with the Irish being significant in the ranching industry in particular well into the mid-twentieth century. Almost every region of the state had Irish ranchers, with many Irish ranches being established in the late nineteenth and early twentieth centuries. Irishmen were prominent in both the cattle and sheep industries.

In some communities, the day was recognized by celebratory parties in the Irish community and in organizations associated with them. In Casper, for example, the Knights of Columbus hosted a St. Patrick's Day party for many years. This is less the case today, but the Irish in Wyoming still are part of the state's cultural heritage.

Irish American Wyomingites have figured prominently in other fields as well and have notably contributed to politics and law in the state. Wyoming has contributed one Irish American, Mike Sullivan, to the ambassadorship to Ireland. Former governor Sullivan was ambassador to Ireland during the Clinton administration.

Sidebar:
The Irish in Wyoming

The Irish are a significant demographic, in terms of ancestry, in the United States in general, so a reader might be justifiably forgiven for thinking that the story of the Irish in Wyoming wouldn't be particularly unique or perhaps even that such an entry must be contrived. This would be far from the case, however, as the Irish were not only an identifiable element in European American settlement of the state but also a distinct one with a unique history.

It may not be possible to tell when the first Irishman or Irish American entered the state, but a pretty good

Bantry Bay, Ireland. Many of central Wyoming's Irish immigrants came from the Bantry Bay area. *Library of Congress.*

guess would be that the very first son of Erin entered what would become the state in the service of the U.S. Army. More particularly, it seems likely that this would have been with the Corps of Discovery, that body of men commissioned by the army to cross the continent from St. Louis to the Pacific Ocean. Sergeant Patrick Gass was definitely of Irish descent, although he himself came from Pennsylvania. He's unique, as he left the first literary work on the expedition. George Shannon was of Irish Protestant descent and, therefore, perhaps Scots-Irish, although his name would suggest otherwise. The corps, however, crossed the continent prior to the great migration caused by the famine, and therefore it's almost surprising that these men of Irish descent were on the expedition, as the Irish were a small demographic at the time. Also revealing, at this time, many, probably most, whose ancestors had come over from Ireland were of Scots-Irish descent, those being descendant from the Scots population that the English had settled in Ireland to form a religious and ethnic barrier between themselves and the native inhabitants of the conquered country.

The fact that the first Irish Americans to enter the region, however, came in the form of soldiers was telling, as by the 1840s this was becoming common. Up until that time, the U.S. Army had been tiny and had very little presence on the frontier at all. The Mexican War, however, changed all that and at the same time brought a flood of Irishmen into the enlisted ranks. This was caused by the contemporaneous jump in emigration from Ireland at the time, which was coincident with a huge spike in German immigration as well. There was a political element to both immigration waves, with the Irish being discontent with the United Kingdom, which disadvantaged them by law with statutes aimed against Catholics, and with some German immigrants coming during the troubled times on the continent that would lead to European-wide revolutions in the 1840s. The Irish in particular, however, were also driven by extreme poverty and hunger, as their disadvantaged state was further compounded by extreme crop failures in this period. Taking leave to the United States or British Canada, many simply chose to get out of Ireland. Upon arriving in the United States, still oppressed by poverty and often just downright oppressed, many took a traditional employment route, which was to enlist in military service. Like their ethnic cousins the Scots, the Irish were not in actuality a particularly martial people, but standing armies provided an economic refuge for them. In the United Kingdom, this resulted in Irish and Scots regiments of the

British army. In the United States, starting during the Mexican War, it resulted in a huge percentage of the enlisted ranks being made up of Irish volunteers.

The Irish and Germans were at first resented in the service, even if their enlistments were accepted, and they were very much looked down upon by southern-born officers, who made up a disproportionate percentage of the army's officer class. This had, in part, sparked a high desertion rate during the Mexican War and even contributed to the formation of a unit in the Mexican army made up of Irish and German desertions, the San Patricios. The army, however, in what might be the first instance of a long U.S. Army tradition of adapting to social change ahead of the general population, made peace with the Irish enlisted men by war's end, and they soon became an enduring feature of the army. By the time of the Civil War, things had changed so much that there were now Irish American and Irish-born officers in the regular army, such as Irish American Philip Sheridan, after whom Sheridan and Sheridan County, Wyoming, are named.

This change started to take place almost as soon as the Mexican War was over and was well established by the time the Civil War broke out. Already by that time, many rank and file members of the army

General Philip Sheridan and staff during the Civil War. Sheridan County and the town of Sheridan, Wyoming, are named for the general, reflecting the common nineteenth-century practice of naming counties and towns after serving army officers of the period. *Library of Congress.*

were Irish born, and there were Irish American officers of note. The controversial Patrick Connor provides one such example, with Connor having a major campaigning role in Wyoming during the Civil War. After the war ended, the post–Civil War U.S. Army was full of Irish and German volunteers. The list of the dead at Little Big Horn reads like an Irish town roster, so heavy was the concentration of the Irish born in its ranks. Indeed, the Irish in the Seventh Cavalry and other U.S. Army units had a permanent impact on American military music during the period, contributing such martial tunes as "Garryowen" and "The Girl I Left Behind Me" to the American military music book.

After Irish soldiers came the Irish railroad workers, who arrived with the construction crews of the Union

Top: General Patrick Connor. *Library of Congress*.

Right: Miles Keogh, an Irishman who served in the British army and the Swiss guards before becoming an officer in the U.S. Army. Keogh's horse, Comanche, is sometimes inaccurately claimed to be the only survivor of Little Big Horn. Even the army, which knew otherwise, promoted this as a myth. *Library of Congress*.

The train station in Medicine Bow. *Photograph by the author.*

Pacific. The role of Irishmen in the construction of the railway is well known. Along with other ethnic minorities, the Irish were strongly represented in the crews that made their way through the state in the late 1860s. As towns came up along the rail line, some of these men would inevitably leave the employment of the railroad and take up residence in other occupations. Cheyenne, Laramie, Medicine Bow, Rawlins, Green River, Rock Springs and Evanston all share this Union Pacific source of origin.

After the railways started to come in, cattle did as well. Rail lines were, in fact, a critical element of the conversion of the United States from a pork-consuming to a beef-consuming country, as rail was needed in order to ship cattle to packinghouses in the Midwest. Rail expanded into Wyoming at exactly that point in time when the greatly expanded herds in Texas started to be driven out of that state. Prior to that time, while beef was certainly consumed, it tended to be a local product, and pig production provided the primary meat source in the United States, along with poultry, fowl and wild game. Texas's cattle had been raised primarily for their hides, not their beef. The Civil War, however, had seen an uncontrolled herd expansion, and at the war's end, the cattle had become a nearly free resource provided a way of sending them to central markets could be found. The expansion of the rail lines soon provided that, and the long trail drive era was born. And with the cattle came some Irish cowhands and, ultimately, Irish ranchers.

Ireland itself was nearly completely dominated by agriculture in the nineteenth century and most of the twentieth. Agriculture was the largest sector of the Irish economy as late as the 1990s. In the nineteenth century, as with every century before that, most Irish were rural and agricultural. Looked at that way, employment in nonagricultural activities really meant that most of the Irishmen taking them up were leaving their natural-born employments for something else.

Moreover, while we today tend to think of Ireland exclusively in terms of potatoes due to the horror of the famine, in reality the Irish have a very long association with horses and cattle. In pre-Christian Ireland, stealing cattle was virtually a national sport, and the great Irish epic work *The Cattle Raid of Cooley* (*Táin Bó Cúailnge*) concerns that activity. In later years, during English occupation, potatoes became an Irish staple because Irish farmers tended to grow them for themselves by necessity while still often working production crops on English-owned lands. Even as late as the famine, Ireland exported wheat to the United Kingdom. Cattle raising never stopped, and indeed, by World War I, Ireland was a significant beef exporter to Great Britain. The same is also true of sheep, which were raised all over Ireland for their wool and meat, giving rise to the idea that all Irish are clad in tweed at all times, a concept that also applies to the sheep-raising Scots.

Horses, for their part, were and remain an Irish national obsession. Unlike the English and Scots, whose routine farmers had little interest in riding stock, the Irish developed an early love of horse riding and everything associated with it. The steeplechase was and is an Irish national sport, followed intensely even now and in earlier eras widely engaged in. A person has to wonder, therefore, if the heavy Irish representation in cavalry formations in the U.S. Army of the nineteenth century reflected that fact. It certainly did in the English army, which had at least one Irish cavalry regiment up until Irish independence.

All this made the Irish a people who were particularly inclined to go into animal husbandry. Other agricultural Europeans, except perhaps the Scots, had less exposure to this sort of agriculture than the Irish did. It's no wonder, therefore, that the Irish were well represented among nineteenth-century cowboys and, ultimately, among small-scale nineteenth- and twentieth-century ranchers.

Cowboys. *Library of Congress.*

Indeed, on more than one occasion, Irish immigrant ranchers were able to convert humble beginnings into enormous agricultural enterprises. One such example was the case of Patrick J. Sullivan, an Irish immigrant who started ranching sheep near Rawlins. As his ranch grew, he moved to Casper and became a wealthy man from sheep ranching, which then translated into politics as he became mayor of Casper and ultimately a U.S. senator upon the death of Francis Warren. Sullivan had come a long way from his humble beginnings in Bantry Bay. His Irish roots were reflected in the balcony of the large house he built in Casper, which featured a shamrock on the banister of the widow's walk, although that feature is now gone.

No story about the Irish in the United States would be complete without noting the role that Irish-born clerics played, as the Irish were always closely identified with the Catholic Church, a fact that ultimately was pivotal in Ireland's independence following World War I. In Wyoming, the presence of the Irish guaranteed the presence of the Catholic Church, and in many areas but not all, Irish-born parishioners and Irish American parishioners were the largest segment of any one congregation. Because the church was essentially a missionary church in Wyoming, it relied for decades on Irish priests. The first bishop of the Diocese of Cheyenne was the Irish-born Maurice Burke, who served from 1887 until 1893 and had to defend his diocese from hostility from nativist elements, which were strong at the time. He was succeeded by Thomas Lenihan, who was also Irish born. Irish-born priests continued to be very common well into the twentieth century and only came to a slow end after World War II, although at least one Irish-born retired priest remains in residence at St. Patrick's in Casper.

In a state where they were fairly strongly represented, it's perhaps not surprising that the Irish were able to have some success in politics even though there remained a strong anti-Catholic prejudice in much of the United States prior to World War I. Indeed, at least according to one source, some early Irish businessmen and politicians in the state made efforts not to make their Catholicism generally well known and were muted about their faith, being aware of the prejudice that existed against it. Nonetheless, as the example of Patrick Sullivan provides, there were successful Irish-born and Irish American politicians in the state fairly early. Sullivan may provide the best early example, but others are provided by mid-twentieth-century politicians Joseph O'Mahoney and Frank Barrett.

An identifiable Irish presence in the state remained through most of the twentieth century, but by the last decade, it had begun to fade as Irish immigrants aged and began to pass on. Some still remain, but the era of Irish immigration to Wyoming is over. Like most of the United States, a residual Irish influence lingers on in subtle ways and in the memories of Irish descendants, many of whom can also claim ancestry from other lands by now. But the impact of the Irish on the state, while not as open and apparent as it once was, continues on and always will, given their significant role in the nineteenth- and twentieth-century history of the state.

1869 Carbon post office is established.

1890 The Sundance Hose Company #1, a fire company (fire department), held a "grand dance." Whether coincidence or not, late nineteenth- and early twentieth-century fire departments and police departments were heavily Irish in many U.S. localities, although I would not have expected that to be the case in Sundance.

March 18

1883 Cheyenne newspapers report on a shocking total of thirty-seven executions within a reportable time frame having been conducted by vigilantes.

1918 The city of Casper reports twenty-two arrests during the weekend, perhaps because of an outbreak of excessively boisterous St. Patrick's Day celebrations.

1921 Spotted Horse post office is established. Spotted Horse was a Crow leader, and the junction is named for him.

1994 The triceratops is adopted as the official state dinosaur.

March 19

1864 Charles Russell is born. The Missouri-born artist would move to Montana at a young age and leave a record of unique and accurate depictions of ranching on the Northern Plains. More even than Remington, his paintings leave us an accurate record of early ranching in Wyoming, Montana and Alberta.

1868 Sioux led by Crazy Horse attack Horsecreek Station, which is on the Wyoming-Nebraska border

March 20

1876 The Chugwater division station on the Cheyenne–Black Hills stage line is established. This is notable to a degree in that another 1876 event, the Battle of Powder River, had just occurred in a year that would later see the Battle of the Rosebud and the Battle of Little Big Horn, showing that the region was far from settled.

1884 Laramie, the "Gem City of the Plains," is incorporated.

1895 An explosion at the Red Canyon Mine in Almy kills sixty-one miners.

March 21

1862 Ben Holladay buys the Russell, Majors & Waddell stage line.

1899 The Wyoming Historical Society Museum in Cheyenne opens.

1954 Cheyenne's KFBC-TV Channel 5 starts broadcasting.

March 22

1881 "Big Nose" George Parrott is lynched in Rawlins. He was being held for murder, and his lynching followed an attempted jailbreak in which he injured jailor Robert Rankin.

1881 The first telephone exchange in Wyoming is established.

2007 Grizzly bears are removed from the endangered species list. Wyoming has a fair number of grizzly bears that have expanded outside Yellowstone National Park, where they had been concentrated at one time.

March 23

1888 Ella Watson, remembered as Cattle Kate, files for the patent on her homestead located on the Sweetwater, near the homestead of Jim Averell.

1942 The U.S. government begins moving Japanese Americans from their West Coast homes to detention centers that would ultimately include Heart Mountain, near Cody.

March 24

1890 The school at St. Stephens opens.

1934 Rodeo promoter, racehorse owner and rancher Charles Irwin's funeral is held in Cheyenne. General Pershing was one of his honorary pallbearers.

Irwin is little recalled today, but he was a major entertainment figure during his lifetime. He is sometimes mentioned as possibly having a role in Tom Horn's attempted escape from the Laramie County Jail, but there's little evidence to suggest that is true, and Irwin never commented on it. His weight climbed enormously in his later years, and as a result, a special coffin had to be built for the five-foot-four, five-hundred-pound Irwin. He died at fifty-nine years of age from injuries sustained in an automobile accident, with the automobile having been driven by his son-in-law.

1939 Earl Durand is killed while robbing a bank in Powell. Durand has been popularized in legend as a latter-day mountain man and the "Tarzan of the Tetons." In reality, he was a Powell-area farm kid with a fair degree of woodcraft knowledge, a not atypical set of regional skills then or later. He was arrested in the early spring of 1939 for poaching but broke out of jail and then took a deputy sheriff and town marshal hostage and forced them to his parents' home, where he killed them. He lived in the mountains for a period of days and then chose to rob the Powell bank for reasons that remain debated.

March 25

1877 Deadwood stage driver and the son of Cheyenne's marshal Johnny Slaughter is killed by outlaws two miles outside Deadwood.

1915 Arminto, Wyoming, is incorporated. Arminto was a major sheep shipping point in the twentieth century, and at one time, more sheep were shipped from its stockyards, where they were loaded onto trains, than from any other place in the world.

Today, with the decline in the American sheep industry, Arminto is nearly a ghost town, with just a few remaining residents. The town's once busy railhead is now just a rail crossing.

March 26

1804 The District of Louisiana, including most of Wyoming, is established by an act of the U.S. Congress.

1890 Territorial delegate Joseph M. Carey introduces a bill calling for statehood for Wyoming.

1918 Elmer Lovejoy of Laramie patents a powered garage door opener. Lovejoy had previously built his own automobile. Clearly, he was a visionary of the first order.

1926 Game and Fish planted twenty-seven pairs of Hungarian partridges. The plant was a success, as "Huns" and Chukars are fairly well established in the state today.

1993 The TA Ranch, scene of the siege of the invaders during the Johnson County War, is added to the National Register of Historic Places.

March 27

1890 The House of Representatives passes the bill for Wyoming statehood.

1909 The trustees of the University of Wyoming fire the university's president.

March 28

1865 The District of the Plains, a military district including Wyoming, is established.

1870 Camp Augur is reorganized and renamed Camp Brown.

1908 Fifty-nine people are killed in a mine explosion at Hanna.

2008 Gray wolves are removed from the endangered species list.

March 29

1879 The Laramie County Stock Growers Association changes its name to the Wyoming Stock Growers Association (WSGA). The WSGA was to be a major political force early in the state's history and was central to its early range laws.

1887 The following soldiers, stationed at posts in Wyoming, earned the Congressional Medal of Honor for action on this day:

Second Lieutenant Lloyd M. Brett, Second U.S. Cavalry. Place and date: O'Fallons Creek, Montana, April 1, 1880. Entered service at: Malden, Massachusetts. Born: February 22, 1856, Dead River, Maine. Date of issue: February 7, 1895. Citation: "Fearless exposure and dashing bravery in cutting off the Indians' pony herd, thereby greatly crippling the hostiles."

Captain Eli L. Huggins, Second U.S. Cavalry. Place and date: O'Fallons Creek, Montana, April 1, 1880. Entered service at: Minnesota. Born: Illinois. Date of issue: November 27, 1894. Citation: "Surprised the Indians in their strong position and fought them until dark with great boldness."

1888 The state capitol is completed.

1906 Construction at Pathfinder Dam suffers a setback due to flood damage.

March 30

1889 Butch Cassidy participates in a bank robbery in Denver with the McCarty brothers.

1891 The Shoshone National Forest is set aside by President Benjamin Harrison as the Yellowstone Park Timberland Reserve.

1909 The U.S. Army abandons Fort Washakie. The post had previously also been known as Camp Brown and Camp Augar. The post had lately been a Ninth Cavalry post, which was an all-black cavalry regiment at this time, since the army was segregated.

The facilities for the post remain in large part today, having gone over to the Bureau of Indian Affairs. Fort Washakie, the town, is the seat of government for the Wind River Indian Reservation. The structures provide good examples of the period stone construction used by the army at that time.

1915 A quarantine on Wyoming livestock is put in place due to an outbreak of hoof and mouth disease.

2009 The Wyoming Range Legacy Act is signed into law by President Obama.

March 31

1888 Elwood Mead, the predominant force in Wyoming's water law to the current day, takes office as state engineer.

1942 Tim McCoy, western actor and Wyoming native, announces his candidacy for the U.S. Senate. His campaign would not be a successful one, and he entered the army for the second time after losing in the primary.

APRIL IN WYOMING

April in Wyoming is a month that sees the struggle between winter's efforts to hang on and spring's efforts to start. As such, it is a month with incredibly volatile weather conditions, swinging between mild summer-like weather and deep wintry weather. Wyoming gets more snow in April than in any other month of the year. It can be a deadly month for stockmen, although it is also a month of brandings for most cattlemen.

The weather played a major role in one of Wyoming's most significant historical events, the Johnson County War, which saw its most dramatic episodes occur in April.

APRIL

Sidebar: The Johnson County War

This dramatic event may be the single most significant in Wyoming's history if measured in terms of popularity. It's been the subject of several books, most recently John W. Davis's *Wyoming Range War*, and it's formed the basic plot outline, in a highly developed and adulterated way, for endless novels and movies, including such famous ones as *The Virginian* (the only one to really take the large stockman's side) and *Shane*. The popular concept of the war is that it represented an armed expression of unadulterated greed. While greed cannot be dismissed as an element, the larger question remains: what was it all about?

The cattle industry as we know it didn't really come about until the conclusion of the Civil War. Prior to that, the most significant meat livestock in the United States was pork. Swine production produced the basic farm meat for most Americans, which is not to say that they didn't eat cattle; they did, but cattle production was fairly small scale in the East, and much of it was focused on dairy and mixed production. Meat cattle were more common in the South, and while it's popular to note that American ranching was a development of Mexican ranching, it was also very much a development of southern ranching practices. This, in fact, partially gave rise to the Johnson County War, as will be seen.

At any rate, the American beef cattle industry was born when the railroads penetrated Kansas after the Civil War and returning Texas cattlemen found that the herds in their state had gone wild and greatly increased. Cattle in Texas up until that time had followed the Mexican practice of being raised principally for their hides, not for meat, but the introduction of rail into Kansas meant that cattle could now be driven, albeit a long ways, to a railhead and then shipped to market. An explosion in urban centers in the East provided a natural market, and soon the cattle industry in Texas had switched over to being focused on shipping cattle for beef.

The Texas industry spread north as well, and by the 1870s, it was making inroads into Wyoming, although really only into southern Wyoming for the most part. At the same time, and often forgotten, a dramatic increase in herds in Oregon, the byproduct of early farm herds and pioneer oxen herds, produced a surplus there that caused herds to be driven back east into Wyoming at the very moment that northern Wyoming opened up for ranching.

But what was ranching like here at the time? It was dominated by the fact of the Homestead Act, a bill passed during the Civil War in order to encourage western migration into the vast public domain. But the bill had been written by men familiar only with eastern farming, and it used the eastern agricultural unit (forty acres) as a model. That amount of acreage was perfectly adequate for a yeoman farmer, and indeed, after the Civil War, "forty acres and a mule" was the dream of liberated slaves, which they hoped to obtain from the federal government. But forty acres wasn't anywhere near adequate for any sort of livestock unit in the West, and most of the West wasn't suitable for farming. In the West, additionally, the federal homesteading provisions oddly dovetailed with state and territorial water law.

Water law was the domain of states or territories exclusively and evolved in the mining districts of California, which accepted that claiming water in one place and moving it to another was a necessary right. This type of water law, much different from that existing in the well-watered East, spread to the West, and a "first in time, first in right" concept of water law evolved. This was to be a significant factor in western homesteading. Additionally, the federal government allowed open use of unappropriated public lands for grazing. States and territories, accepting this system, sought to organize the public grazing by district, and soon an entire legal system evolved that accepted the homesteading of a small acreage, usually for the control of water, and the use of vast surrounding public areas, perhaps collectively but under the administration of some grazing body, some of which, particularly in Wyoming, were legally recognized. In the case of Wyoming, the Wyoming Stock Growers Association controlled the public grazing and had quasi-legal status in that livestock detectives who policed the system were recognized by law as stock detectives.

This was the system that the large ranching interests accepted, developed and became used to in the 1870s and 1880s. Large foreign corporations bought into western ranching, accepting that this was in fact the system. It had apparent legal status.

But nothing made additional small homesteading illegal. And the penalty for failing to cooperate in the grazing districts mostly amounted to being shunned or having no entry into annual roundups. This continued to encourage some to file small homesteads. Homesteading was actually extremely expensive, and it was difficult for many to do much more than file. Ironically, small homesteading was aided by the large ranchers' practice of paying good hands partially in livestock, giving them the ability to start up where they otherwise would not have been able. It was the dream of many top hands, even if it had not been when they first took up employment as cowboys, to get a large enough, albeit small, herd together and start out on their own. Indeed, if they hoped to marry, and most men did, they had little choice, the only other option being to get out of ranch work entirely, as the pay for a cowhand was simply not great enough to allow for very many married men to engage in it.

By the 1880s, this was beginning to cause a conflict between the well-established ranchers, who tended to be large, and the newer ones, who tended to be small. The large stockmen were distressed by the carving up of what they regarded as their range, with some justification, and sought to combat it by legal means. One such method was the exclusion of smaller stockmen from the large regional roundups, which were done collectively at that time and were fairly controlled events. Exclusion from a roundup could be very problematic for a small stockman grazing on the public domain, as they all were, and this forced them into smaller, unofficial roundups. Soon, this created the idea that they were engaging in theft. To make matters even more problematic, Wyoming and other areas attempted to combat this through "Maverick" laws, which allowed any unbranded, un–cow attended calf to be branded with the brand of its discoverer. This law, it was thought, would allow large stockmen to claim the strays found on their ranges that they assumed, because of their larger herds, to be theirs (a not unreasonable assumption), but in fact the law actually encouraged theft, as it allowed anybody with a brand to brand a calf, unattended or not, as long as nobody was watching. Soon, a situation developed in which large stockmen were convinced that smaller stockmen were acting illegally or semi-illegally and that certain areas of the state were controlled by thieves or near thieves, while the small stockmen rightly regarded their livelihoods as being under siege. Soon, they'd be under de facto siege.

This forms the backdrop of the Johnson County War. Yes, it represented an effort by the landed and large to preserve what they had against the small entrant. But their belief that they were acting within the near confines of the law, if not solidly within it, was not wholly irrational. They convinced themselves that their opponents were all thieves, but their belief that they were protecting a recognized legal system, or nearly protecting it, had some basis in fact. This is not to excuse their efforts, but from their perspective, the breakup of recognized grazing districts by small entrants was an obvious threat to its existence (and, indeed, it would come to an end), and the Maverick laws were protecting what they had conceived of as a legal right. Their opponents, for that matter, were largely acting within the confines of the law as well and naturally saw the attack as motivated by greed.

As with many things, the conflict in systems of laws gave each side a basis to see its own acts as fully valid. The small stockmen had the high side of the fight, but the fight itself was more ambiguous in motivations, to some degree, than is typically portrayed.

The fight didn't start with the invasion at all, but actually a campaign of assassinations was started by somebody. It cannot be assumed that the WSGA had ratified this, but certainly whoever commenced it was on that side of the fight. It proved unsuccessful, and if anything, it made Johnson County residents nervous but all the more opposed to those aligning against them. Finally, as we have seen, events transpired to the point where the WSGA actually sponsored an invasion, albeit one of the most ineptly planned and executed ones ever conducted by anyone.

The invasion, as we've seen, was a total failure in terms of execution. It succeeded in taking the lives of two men, with some loss of life on its part as well, but it did nothing to address the perceived problem it was intended to address. The invaders were much more successful in avoiding the legal implications of their acts through brilliant legal maneuvering on the part of their lawyers, but the act of attempting the invasion brought so much attention to their actions that they effectively lost the war by losing the public relations aspect of it. For the most part, the men involved in it were able to continue on in their occupations without any ill effect on those careers—a fairly amazing fact under the circumstances—and outside of Governor Barber, whose political career was destroyed, even the political impacts of the invasion were only temporary. Willis Van Devanter was even able to go on to serve on the United States Supreme Court, in spite of the unpopularity of his clients in the defense of the matter. Violence continued on for some time, however, with some killings, again engaged in with unknown sponsors, occurring. However, not only a change in public opinion occurred but soon a change in perceived enemies occurred as well, and a new range war would erupt against a new enemy: sheep. The range itself would continue to be broken up unabated until the Taylor Grazing Act was passed early in Franklin Roosevelt's administration, which saved the range from further homesteading and ultimately led to a reconsolidation of much of the range land.

April 1

Frank Canton. *Courtesy of Wyoming State Archives, Department of State Parks and Cultural Resources.*

1887 Frank Canton becomes the chief stock detective for northern Wyoming.

1892 The *New York Times* reports that (large) Wyoming stockmen have launched a raid that would become known as the Johnson County War. This date is remarkable in that it predates the first assault of the war and shows how plans had already broken as news even at the point the raid was just starting. The *New York Times* article featured a headline that read: "OUT FOR WHOLESALE LYNCHINGS; WYOMING CATTLEMEN ON A CAMPAIGN AGAINST THIEVES."

1915 Wyoming's workers' compensation act goes into effect. Workers' compensation fits into the category of economic news that most people find terminally dull, but this was a landmark in Wyoming's history. The much-maligned workers' compensation system is actually highly unique, and Wyoming was a very early adopter of this type of system.

An entirely state-administered system, completely occupying the field, it was modeled on the German workers' compensation system, which was the origin of the German national healthcare system. Like the German system, Wyoming's makes the state the insurer of covered workers rather than requiring employers to purchase private workers' compensation insurance. The system is also quasi-judicial in nature, having an adjudicatory system for contested claims with a right of appeal to the state's court system.

The system also directly impacts civil litigation in Wyoming, as it prohibits suits against employers where an employee has received benefits under the act. Suits against co-employees are allowed but only under a very heightened standard.

1918 It was reported that by this day, for a period dating back to December 1, 1917, Wyoming's revenues from oil royalties had increased 74 percent, an effect, no doubt, of World War I.

1951 The Wyoming Air National Guard's Eighty-seventh Fighter Squadron was activated for service during the Korean Conflict, with personnel assigned to Clovis Air Force Base, New Mexico; Germany; Okinawa; and South Korea. Wyoming pilots would fly 1,800 missions during the Korean War.

April 2

1870 An Indian attack on the Sweetwater kills six settlers.

1881 Big Nose George Parrott is sentenced to death.

1892 George Dunning, an intimate of the conspirators associated with the invasion of Johnson County, returned from Idaho to Cheyenne at the behest of H.B. Ijams, secretary of the Wyoming Stock Growers Association, to participate in the raid, although he professed disapproval. He drew a .45-90 Winchester from a Cheyenne store where accounts had been set up to arm the invaders. While the plot did not yet have the endorsement of the WSGA, it was well advanced by WSGA officials at the time.

1909 The Spring Creek Raid marks the last open attack in a long-running range war in Wyoming and concludes the era of private warfare in the state. In the Spring Creek Raid, a collection of Big Horn County cattlemen attacked sheepman Joe Allemand, killed him and then burned his sheepwagon. This was one of a series of such raids that had occurred since sheep were introduced into Wyoming in the 1890s. The brutality of the assault shocked area residents, who for the first time supported legal efforts to prosecute the perpetrators in the Big Horn Basin, which previously had not been the case. The tide had effectively shifted some years earlier in much of the state, as the willingness to prosecute and execute assassin Tom Horn in 1903 had demonstrated.

As news traveled more slowly in those days, news of the attack was first published in Natrona County, Wyoming, on April 6, 1909.

1948 A fire destroys thirty Laramie businesses.

April 3

1860 The Pony Express service begins between St. Joseph, Missouri, and San Francisco, California. In Wyoming, the mail route followed the Oregon Trail.

I have to note that starting this in the month of April, given the weather on the Plains, was odd.

1863 Utes attack the station garrisoned by the Sixth Ohio Cavalry at Sweetwater, Utah.

1868 A wood-cutting party near Rock Creek is attacked by Indians.

April 4

1872 The Wyoming Stock Growers Association is officially organized.

1906 Worland is incorporated.

1916 Bill Carlisle robs passengers on the UP's Overland Limited as it travels between Laramie and Cheyenne.

Bill Carlisle (right) and Carbon County sheriff Rubie Rivera. Carlisle, in spite of being a train robber, was very widely liked by most people who knew him, which this photo somewhat reflects. While in the Wyoming State Penitentiary in Rawlins, he underwent a religious conversion and converted to Catholicism. After his release, he led a model life. *Courtesy of Wyoming State Archives, Department of State Parks and Cultural Resources.*

April 5

1892 A specially chartered train leaves Denver, Colorado, for Cheyenne carrying hired Texas gunmen bound ultimately for central Wyoming. The train would pick up large stockmen associated with the WSGA in Cheyenne before going on to Casper. This was the opening phase in the Johnson County War, the best known, if not particularly accurately remembered, of the range wars on the Northern Plains.

April 6

1808 John Jacob Astor incorporates the American Fur Company. Not in Wyoming, of course, which didn't exist by that name at the time, but the company would have an influence on the early history of the state.

1860 The first westbound Pony Express arrives at Fort Laramie.

1892 A special train carrying the "invaders," hired gunmen and representatives of large cattle interests, arrives in Casper and discharges its passengers under darkness at about 4:00 a.m. The chartered train arrived with its window shades drawn, but the secrecy associated with it only encouraged rumors about its cargo. The men traveled a few miles north of Casper and assembled at Casper Creek at about 9:00 a.m. Delays soon set in, with horses breaking free and requiring hours to be rounded up. Some horses were never found, and the men whose mounts those were rode in wagons. As it had snowed, traveling by wagon proved slow. The party made twenty miles that day.

For perspective, a typical long day for an Oregon Trail party was about thirty miles, although many days were shorter. The cavalry of the period typically made thirty miles a day, although they could go farther.

April 7

1870 Residents of Miner's Delight, led by Captain (from the Civil War) Herman G. Nickerson, attack a band of Arapaho led by Black Bear, killing fourteen. The raid had intended to intercept and attack a party of Arapaho under Little Shield, who had attacked two residents of Miner's Delight the day prior. Tension between locals and Arapahos on the Wind River Reservation had been high for several months. Black Bear's band, however, had merely been on its way to Camp Brown to trade.

1892 Dissension comes to a head in the Johnson County invasion, resulting in Frank Wolcott resigning command of the expedition and ceding it to Tom Smith and Frank Canton, with Smith "commanding" the Texans. To add to their difficulties, a heavy snowstorm broke out. The party broke into two groups, with some men becoming lost in the process, including Wolcott, who spent the night in a haystack as a result.

1922 Ground is broken for the town of Parco. Parco still exists but is now known as Sinclair and is the site of the Sinclair Refinery. At the time of its founding, it was the location of a very nice hotel on the Lincoln Highway. The hotel's buildings still exist, but the hotel itself is long closed.

1922 The U.S. secretary of interior leases Naval Reserve #3, "Teapot Dome," in Wyoming to Harry F. Sinclair.

1933 Prohibition is repealed for beer of no more than 3.2 percent alcohol by weight.

April 8

1890 An election for the county seat of Natrona County pits Casper against Bessemer. Bessemer received more votes but had only twenty-four residents, so the commissioners ruled the vote fraudulent and chose Casper as the county seat. Bessemer no longer exists.

1892 On the afternoon of this day, a stock detective and invader informed the invasion party at the Tisdalde Ranch that "rustlers" were located at the KC Ranch and that the party included Nate Champion, a well-known and somewhat controversial small stockman. Stockmen Irvine and Wolcott urged an immediate march on the location, which perhaps was not surprising, as Champion was a witness against stockman enforcer Joe Elliot. Canton, Ford, Campbell and Hesse, however, urged the party to march on to Buffalo, which was regarded as the headquarters of the opposition (and which demonstrates how bold the stockmen's plan really was). After drinking and arguing, a vote was taken, and the party elected to march on the KC. The Johnson County invaders reached the KC Ranch in Johnson County, Wyoming, at midnight. Since disembarking in Casper on April 6, they had ridden east and then north, cutting telegraph lines in the process.

In modern highway miles, the trip is only about seventy miles. Granted, in the context of the era, that would be a fairly long distance to cover by horse, so perhaps the amount of time that the invading party took to cover this distance is not too surprising. A typical cavalry unit at the time covered about thirty miles in a day, although they could cover sixty or more, while severely stressing their mounts, if necessary. Here, as the invading party was entering clearly hostile terrain, depleting their mounts unnecessarily would have been unwise.

Having said that, the amount of time that this advance took was significant in that it showed the extraordinarily ill-advised nature of the expedition. It took the party nearly two days to reach their first target, and they had yet to deeply penetrate into Johnson County. The presence of the party was already known, and counterinsurgents, if you will, were already at work preventing the telegraph lines that the invaders had taken down from being repaired. While their location had not yet been discovered, a better military mind would have regarded them as already in a poor tactical posture. Worse yet for their endeavor, new articles had been published in Cheyenne, Denver and New York to the effect that an action was afoot. Cheyenne's newspaper even correctly noted that their specially chartered train had gone through Douglas and Casper and then discharged its passengers for a trip to Johnson County.

1903 President Theodore Roosevelt commences his 1903 visit of Wyoming, starting with sixteen days in Yellowstone National Park. His total time in Wyoming for the trip would be nineteen days. Much of that time was spent on horseback.

April 9

1884 An elderly Shoshone woman whose grave marker lists her as Sacajawea dies on the Wind River Reservation. She almost certainly was not, but at the time of this woman's death, there were those championing that idea, and some still adhere to it.

1890 F.E. Warren is inaugurated as the first governor of the state of Wyoming. Warren was a Civil War recipient of the Medal of Honor and would shortly become Wyoming's senator. His daughter married John F. Pershing, and his name was later given to Cheyenne's Warren Air Force Base, which was first Fort F.E. Warren. He is not wholly without controversy, as he was closely associated with the WSGA at the time of the invasion, and it is fairly clear that he had at least some tangential involvement with the events of that time. His association with the events nearly cost him his senatorial seat.

1890 The government conducts an auction of buildings and furniture at Fort Laramie.

1892 The siege of the Champion cabin at the KC Ranch commences at 4:00 a.m. when the men build sagebrush fires for heat near the point of their intended assault. The invasion was already going badly, as in the three days since it had commenced, it had advanced only fifty miles and taken no action other than to rip down a series of telegraph lines, a tactic that would be adopted by its opponents, who would take it up to keep the news of the failure of the action from spreading later. Weather was playing a factor, as snow caught the imported Texas gunmen off guard, as they had not dressed for winter (April still being a winter month in Wyoming). The siege at the KC would last all day in spite of the defenders numbering only three men, only one of whom was wanted by the invaders. The invaders numbered about fifty. The invaders ultimately killed Nate

Nate Champion on horse (far left) and his brother Dudley (far right). The wagon is a chuck wagon. Nate was a small rancher in Johnson County on whom the invaders focused as a rustler, although he really simply seems to have been a vocal small rancher. *Courtesy of Wyoming State Archives, Department of State Parks and Cultural Resources.*

Champion, who was one of their prime opponents by their reasoning, but the end of the action would see an invader casualty as well when one of them suffered an ultimately fatal gunshot wound when his horse objected to his mounting. As the rider was grossly overweight, the Wyoming cow pony blew up upon his attempt to remount, ultimately throwing the rider and taking off his rifle at the same time, which discharged. Nick Ray, who was at the Champion cabin at the time of the assault, was also killed in the battle. Two trappers who were present were basically removed from the fighting.

April 10

1803 Napoleon tells his treasury minister that he is considering selling Louisiana to the United States.

1892 The news of the invasion spreads in Johnson County, and the local population begins to react. Jack Flagg, after having nearly been caught by the invaders, rode north spreading the news. The invaders soon received news themselves that residents of the county were in alarm and armed men were on the way to counter them. An argument ensued over whether to take refuge at the TA Ranch and hole up in anticipation of an assault by Johnson County residents—and in order to wait for anticipated relief from federal troops from Fort McKinney—or to proceed with the attack and head to Buffalo. In the meantime, a posse led by Sheriff "Red" Angus arrived at the KC and found the dead bodies of Nate Champion and Nick Ray and that the Nolan cabin, which had been leased by Champion, had been fired. They then returned to Buffalo, a round trip of 120 miles. The Johnson County invaders began to dig in and fortify at the TA Ranch. The invaders suffered two defections who rode off toward Buffalo on their Western Union–leased horses. They were arrested in Buffalo. One of the men had been a reporter and was released when Major Fechet, from Fort McKinney, vouched for him. In the meantime, Flagg and forty-nine men had traveled to the TA.

The events of April 10 are illuminating in showing how badly led the expedition was. In the several days that had passed since the invaders disembarked in Casper, they had been delayed by weather near Casper and had only managed to launch an assault on the Champion cabin. In spite of grossly outnumbering the cabin defenders, defeating Champion had taken all day, and the decision to attack the cabin, and Champion's stalwart defense of it, resulted in the invading party losing a critical day. Their leased horses were being depleted, rumors were rife about what was going on and their presence had been discovered in Johnson County near the southern end. Authorities in Buffalo and Johnson County residents, on the other hand, were reacting swiftly. Sheriff Angus, unlike the invaders, managed to ride to the Champion cabin and back, a whopping 120-mile round trip, and put together a posse inside twenty-four hours. Johnson County residents, for their part, managed to actually form an ad hoc armed band equally as large as the invading party and, by the end of this day, besiege the invaders.

1909 News of the Spring Creek raid hits the papers.

April 11

1803 Napoleon's treasury minister offers to sell Louisiana for $15 million.

1890 Natrona County is organized.

1892 The siege at the TA Ranch has fully set in, with Johnson County residents moving the siege line slowly forward by advancing bales of hay and while pounding the buildings with rifle fire. Heavy rifles, including a .45-145, a heavy "buffalo" rifle, were employed to fire on the structures. One invader made his escape, but the rest were holed up. An effort by twenty invaders to saddle their horses resulted in several horses being shot. A couple men were lightly wounded. A snowfall continued all day and into the night, making the night bright. The Johnson County men asked for the loan of a cannon from Fort McKinney but were refused.

1964 A dedication is held for the copper-plated tyrannosauruses Rex built by S.H. Knight at the University of Wyoming. The life-size dinosaur statue is located just outside the entrance of the Geology Museum at the S.H. Knight Building on campus.

1996 Jessica Dubroff, age seven, and her father and flight instructor die when their airplane crashes after takeoff from Cheyenne Regional in a storm. Dubroff was attempting to be the youngest person to fly across the United States at the time.

April 12

1892 An invader by the name of Dowling, having escaped the TA at night on the eleventh, reaches Douglas, over one hundred miles away, and sends a telegraph to Governor Barber that the invaders are in trouble. Barber had been in on the plot and participated to the extent that he was not going to activate the guard to intervene. Barber asked for the president to intervene, claiming, "An insurrection exists in Johnson County." The telegram to the president did not get through, however, and he then began to telegram Senators Warren and Carey. Carey spoke to the president after being reached that evening, and President Harrison ordered General Brooke in Omaha to send troops. Troops at Fort McKinney were ordered to move and departed in the middle of the night. During the day, the besiegers constructed and began to use a hastily fortified wagon to move their lines closer to the ranch house and barn.

1905 The Wyoming Wool Growers Association is founded.

1934 Harry Sinclair purchases Parco.

2013 Soldiers of the Wyoming Army National Guard's 133rd Engineering Company deploy to Bahrain.

The town of Parco was founded by the Producers and Refiners Corporation as the site of its refinery. The town, which featured this Spanish architecture hotel, was a unique company town with distinct architecture, some of which remains today. *Photograph by the author.*

April 13

1863 General Patrick Connor sends a telegram to General Halleck asking for cavalry reinforcements following a Ute attack at Sweetwater. Ute raids were unusual in Wyoming, and Connor accused the Mormons of urging them on in his message to Halleck.

1892 The Sixth Cavalry arrives from Fort McKinney to intervene in the Johnson County War, which saw large cattle interests "invade" Natrona and Johnson Counties. The Sixth Cavalry was dispatched in response to a request from Wyoming's governor, Barber, who was sympathetic to the invaders, to the effect that "a state of insurrection exists in Johnson County." Upon arriving at the scene, the senior officer on location quickly deduced that the invaders were the offending party and that they were about to be overrun. Rather than allow this to occur, the invaders were arrested.

At the time the Sixth Cavalry arrived, the invaders were in serious danger of being blown to bits, as the Johnson County improvised armored wagon was getting closer and closer to their structures and soon would have been within dynamite-throwing range. They were taken to Fort McKinney.

April 14

1892 Sheriff Angus asks the commander of Fort McKinney to turn over the Johnson County invaders to his custody. The *New York Times* ran Governor Barber's plea for federal troops on its first page.

1902 J.C. Penney and partners opened his first store in Kemmerer. It was a Golden Rule store.

1922 The Tea Pot Dome scandal breaks in the *Wall Street Journal*.

1994 The final Environmental Impact Statement leading to the reintroduction of wolves to Yellowstone National Park is published.

Soldiers with a wolf, Yellowstone National Park. For many years, the park was patrolled by the United States Army, as the U.S. National Park Service did not exist. Even now, the army's role is still recalled in the park service's uniform, which was closely based on the army's at the time it came into existence. Wolves were regarded as a scourge everywhere in the West, and the United States employed "wolfers," whose sole job was to eradicate them. *U.S. Army photograph.*

April 15

1892 Governor Barber requests that Colonel Van Horn of the U.S. Army "obtain the custody of and take to Fort McKinney and there give protection to the men belonging to the invading party who were arrested before the surrender, and who are now confined in the county-jail at Buffalo."

1922 Wyoming Democratic senator John Kendrick introduces a resolution to investigate oil sales at Teapot Dome, Wyoming (the Naval Petroleum Oil Reserve).

April 16

1922 The Teapot Dome scandal is revealed by Senate investigators.

1969 Medicine Wheel is designated as a site on the National Register of Historic Places.

April 17

1944 Wyoming's legislature considers a bill to allow servicemen serving overseas to vote in the general election. Bills of this type were significant enough that Bill Mauldin, author of the famous World War II *Stars and Stripes* cartoon *Up Front*, drew a cartoon regarding it.

April 18

1887 Shakespearean actor Edwin Booth appears in *Hamlet* in Cheyenne.

April 19

1859 Camp Walbach, in present-day Laramie County, is abandoned. It had been occupied by two companies of the Fourth Artillery.

1865 The Eleventh Kansas Cavalry establishes temporary quarters six miles from Platte Bridge Station, Wyoming, at Camp Dodge, which was a tent camp. It had arrived in order to relieve Companies A, B, C and D of the Eleventh Ohio Volunteer Cavalry, which was mustering out. Other companies of the Eleventh Ohio Volunteer Cavalry were to remain.

1877 Crazy Horse (Tȟašúŋke Witkó) and his followers, numbering two thousand warriors, surrender. Crazy Horse had spent much, probably the overwhelming majority, of his free life in Wyoming, although he widely ranged, as would be expected, throughout the region. He was present at the Grattan "Massacre" in 1854, at which time he would have been about fourteen years old. He is believed to have participated in the Fetterman Fight and the Wagon Box Fight. He was a notable figure at the Battle of Little Big Horn, fought in 1876. His 1877 surrender shows how far Sioux and Cheyenne fortunes had declined in less than a year.

1922 Hell's Half Acre is withdrawn from homesteading, although it's difficult to imagine anyone homesteading it.

April 20

1890 The last soldiers leave Fort Laramie.

1920 Caroline Lockhart, attorney Ernest J. Goppert Sr., Princeton-educated dude rancher Irving H. "Larry" Larom, Sid Eldred, Clarence Williams and William Loewert meet to organize the Cody Stampede rodeo. The use of the term "rodeo" was intentionally avoided, as the group thought it sounded too much like a dude word, which was somewhat ironic as at least Lockhart and Larom were transplants who had profited from western romanticism. Goppert was an attorney who would practice in Cody for many decades and was active in Cody affairs.

April 21

1871 Convicted murderer John Boyer is hanged in Laramie, the first Wyomingite to be legally hanged.

April 22—Earth Day

1918 Two men are tarred and feathered for refusing to buy Liberty Bonds in Frontier. World War I, far more than any other twentieth-century American war, saw widespread shunning and hostility toward those who opposed it. Actions of this type were not uncommon, but probably more effective yet was the giving of feathers to young men opposed to the war by young women, indicating to them that the women regarded them as cowards. Statements regarded as sedition were also prosecuted in some states under state law. As an added factor to this, two groups of Americans, those of recent German extraction and those of recent Irish extraction, entered into this era with a degree of cultural hostility toward the English that they had to rapidly overcome, given the spirit of the times.

April 23

1892 The *New York Times* reports on the Johnson County War: "The evidence is said to implicate more than twenty prominent stockmen of Cheyenne whose names have not been mentioned heretofore, also several wealthy stockmen of Omaha, as well as to compromise men high in authority in the State of Wyoming. They will all be charged with aiding and abetting the invasion, and warrants will be issued for the arrest of all of them."

1903 More than two thousand people gather in Newcastle to hear President Theodore Roosevelt speak.

April 24

1903 Theodore Roosevelt dedicates a new stone archway at the entrance to Yellowstone National Park.

April 25

1898 The governor is informed that Wyoming is to provide a battalion of infantry for the war with Spain.

1903 President Theodore Roosevelt visits Newcastle, Wyoming.

1984 The most severe spring blizzard to ever hit Wyoming starts. It would last for three days.

April 26

1886 The University of Wyoming's trustees meet for the first time.

1938 The Como Bluff Dinosaurium is run in *Ripley's Believe It or Not!*

1944 Wyoming's legislature votes to allow deployed soldiers to vote absentee in Wyoming's elections.

April 27

1888 The first Wyoming Arbor Day is proclaimed. Arbor Day is a holiday that was founded in neighboring treeless Nebraska, and while there are those who observe it in Wyoming, it isn't as well observed.

April 28

1868 Negotiations at Fort Laramie commence with the goal of ending Red Cloud's War.

April 29

1868 The Treaty of 1868 is signed, creating the Great Sioux Reservation. The U.S. Army agreed to abandon forts on the Bozeman Trail.

1960 Fort Laramie is designated a site on the National Register of Historic Places.

April 30

1803 The treaty providing for the sale of Louisiana, including most of what would become Wyoming, is signed.

1926 The cornerstone is laid for the University of Wyoming's engineering building.

MAY IN WYOMING

May is the true onset of spring in Wyoming. By May, the late brandings are concluded now that nicer weather has arrived, although many people have been branding since April. Sportsmen are able to get out to the high country really for the first time, while a few stalwarts might still attempt one last cross-country skiing run in the high country.

May 1

1868 Martha Jane Cannary, "Calamity Jane," arrives in Fort Bridger.

1883 William F. Cody puts on his first Wild West Show.

1903 Basin is incorporated.

1909 Cheyenne replaces its volunteer fire department with a full-time paid department.

1920 It is announced that Cheyenne will become a principal stop on the new U.S. Air Mail service route.

May 2

1898 Wyoming National Guard companies activated for service in the Philippines are ordered to report to Camp Richards near Cheyenne.

1905 Construction begins on the rail line from Casper to Lander.

May 3

1881 The grounds of Camp Stambaugh are transferred to the Department of the Interior.

1885 The post hospital opens at Fort Fetterman.

1898 All the Wyoming units mustered for service in the Philippines assemble in Laramie County.

1933 Nellie Tayloe Ross becomes the director of the mints, an office she would hold until 1953.

1946 A military tribunal in Tokyo begins war crimes trials. One of the principal Japanese defendants was defended by Cheyenne lawyer George Guy.

1968 Colorado Air National Guard 120th Tactical Fighter Squadron, flying F-100Cs, becomes the first Air Guard unit to arrive in Vietnam.

1980 The first Wyoming History Day is celebrated.

May 4

1870 First Lieutenant Charles Stambaugh, Second U.S. Cavalry, for whom Camp Stambaugh was named, is killed in action near Miner's Delight.

1925 A contract is awarded for the construction of Guernsey Dam.

1934 The Civilian Conservation Corps establishes Camp Miller near Gillette.

May 5

Today is Cinco de Mayo. The day celebrates the first battle of La Puebla in 1862, in which Mexican forces defeated a French force during Mexico's efforts to oust French-supported Maximilian. The day is not widely celebrated in Mexico, which recognizes a different day as its independence day from Spain, but it has become widely celebrated in the United States.

Sidebar: Hispanics in Wyoming

When I wrote about the Irish, I noted that we could not really determine when the first Irish American or Irishman set foot in what became Wyoming. We can't really do that with Hispanics either, but we can say that Wyoming was once owned by Spain, even if the Spanish were not able to extend the control of their empire in North America as far as they claimed. Indeed, southern Colorado was really the northernmost extent of Spain's empire inside the continent, in spite of occasional claims otherwise. Trade goods did make it farther north, and the Corps of Discovery reported encountering Spanish mules being used by the Shoshones when they came through northern Wyoming. At any rate, not only the Spanish Mexican colony's province of Texas was part of what would become Wyoming, but Spain also once owned Louisiana, and Napoleon's transfer of that territory to the United States required a formal transfer of the territory back to France, which all occurred on the same day, oddly enough.

The transfer of Louisiana to the United States did see a population transfer as well but not one that directly impacts our story here. Louisiana included both a French and a Spanish population who became subject to the United States with the Louisiana Purchase, but the Spanish population did not have a presence in Wyoming at the time. This remained the case in 1836, when Texas, which retained title to a southern portion of what would become Wyoming, rebelled against Mexico. And it remained the case at the time the United States and Mexico concluded the peace Treaty of Guadalupe Hidalgo.

The Mexican War, however, would be directly responsible for the first Hispanic settlers in Wyoming, as it brought the U.S. Army into Wyoming. Only shortly after the war ended, the United States sent the Regiment of Mounted Rifles to occupy what had been a private fort in Wyoming in order to secure part of the early Oregon Trail. That fort was Fort Laramie, which would go on to have one of the most significant roles of any frontier fort in the West. When the army occupied Fort Laramie, its structures were worn and the post was inadequate for its task. Therefore, the army immediately took to rebuilding the post.

Frontier army posts are often imagined to be made up of log buildings surrounded by log stockades, and some were indeed just like that. Only a minority of them, however, had that construction. Some of the posts, in contrast, were surprisingly substantial and well constructed. Fort Laramie was one of these. In its early days as a fur company trading post, it was not much more than a simple stockade, but as soon as the army began to occupy it, that changed. Part of that change was brought about by the importation of Mexican labor from New Mexico. And that had to do with cement.

Cement as a construction material dates back to the Romans. In spite of that, however, it was little used in much of the Western world following the fall of Rome until the late nineteenth century, which in part is due to the manufacturing process becoming somewhat obscure and in part because the types of cement that were commonly known following Rome's decline were slow setting and somewhat hard to make. Therefore, in the mid-nineteenth century, cement was uncommon in the United States. However, for reasons unknown to me, cement remained a construction material elsewhere in the world, including the Spanish world. While it's popular to imagine everything in New Mexico of this era as being constructed of adobe bricks, in fact, cement was a common construction material. With the occupation of New Mexico by the U.S. Army during the Mexican War, this fact became known to the army, which was impressed with cement. So when the army went to reconstruct Fort Laramie, it determined to use cement for the new buildings, which in turn required the importation of laborers who knew how to make it and build with it. Those laborers were New Mexican Hispanics.

These laborers were, therefore, brought up by the army in the late 1840s, and they gave Wyoming its first Hispanic residents. The men brought up, who brought up their families, were not men who were employed year round in New Mexico as construction laborers, as the area was agrarian and such skills were only part of a set of skills used by agrarian artisans. Once they completed their task, therefore, they turned to another part of their skill set: farming. Through this process, not only did Wyoming receive its first Hispanic immigrants, but farming also came to the state for the first time.

The Hispanic farms created by the New Mexican ("Mexican") artisans were located some distance away from the fort on a series of hills visible from the Oregon Trail. The area came be known as Mexican Hills. The Mexican farmers who located there used the presence of the trail for market purposes, selling fresh vegetables to travelers.

I wish I could relate more of this aspect of the story, but unfortunately, I cannot. The area remains farm ground today, but as far as I know, none of the original Mexican presence remains. When it ceased I cannot say either, but my suspicion is that it was during the mid-nineteenth century. With the fort becoming an increasingly important regional center, it may also have become an increasingly difficult place to live. The farmers did not live on the post grounds but some distance from it, and therefore, they would have been at the mercy of Fort Laramie bands of Indians, who were generally peaceful while in the region but would have been somewhat concerning nonetheless. At any rate, I'm not aware of the farms surviving into the twentieth century and have no idea how long they actually lasted. Therefore, I can only sadly report the New Mexican immigrants as the first appearance of Hispanic culture in the state, but whether their presence had any long-lasting cultural impact, I cannot say. It certainly had a long-lasting material impact, however, as the concrete structures built at the fort all still remain, albeit as ruins. That's a lot more than a person can say about the stick-frame buildings that the army generally constructed at its more permanent facilities in the same era.

The next significant presence of Hispanics in the state came about due to the explosion of the cattle industry following the Civil War. In terms of time, that's not really that long after the establishment of the Mexican Hills farms mentioned earlier, and a person has to wonder if any residents still remained. Be that as it may, it's commonly noted that one-third of all nineteenth-century cowboys were black or Mexican. I've always found that description rather odd, as African Americans and Hispanics of the same era had distinctly different cultural histories. Additionally, as they are lumped together by this description, there's no easy way to know what percentage of that one-third were Hispanic. But what is certain is that Texas ranching came about due to ranching in Mexican Texas and dated back to Spanish Texas, so the Mexican influence on the industry was enormous. It's no wonder that Hispanic Texans and New Mexicans remained employed in it up into the 1860s and 1870s and beyond—indeed, to this very day.

The state, therefore, saw new Hispanic men who came up with the herds from Texas. Undoubtedly, some stayed when the long trail drives gave way to regional ranching. Oddly, however, it's hard to find examples of individual Hispanic ranchers. There probably were some, but I'm unaware of them. In terms of ranching methods and technology, of course, their impact was huge and has been enduring throughout the West. Indeed, Wyoming's cowboys were the direct descendants in terms of methods of the *vaquero* who had employed the same skill set in Texas, as opposed to the *caballero* who employed a somewhat different skill set in California. This remains true today.

Mexican ranching influence extended not only to cattle ranching but to sheep ranching as well. The Spanish had introduced sheep to Mexico, and they were a presence in the Southwest before the Mexican War. Sheep started arriving on the Wyoming ranges in the 1890s, accompanied by a great deal of controversy and violence. They were also accompanied by "Mexican herders." Not all sheepherders were of Mexican ancestry by any means. Still, in the very early sheep industry on the Northern Plains,

Mexican influence was strong. Mexican herders were accustomed to highly nomadic herdsmanship, which in part leaned on skills acquired from Indians. While today we are used to the sheepwagon, the "home

A sheep camp advertisment on the former Kistler Tent & Awning Building in downtown Casper, Wyoming. The business still exists but not in this location. *Photograph by the author.*

on the range," Mexican herders used teepees made of canvas. This practice is not well known to those outside the sheep industry, but it was common enough with Mexican herders that the practice lived on well into the twentieth century.

At about the same time that the first herds of cattle began to head north, the Union Pacific came into the state. Hispanic laborers were not part of that rail expansion, but by the early twentieth century, they were very much a major segment of the Union Pacific workforce, and they remain so to this day. All the towns on the Union Pacific came to have significant Hispanic populations. This saw the creation of distinctly Hispanic neighborhoods in all those towns, which reflects on the human nature in good and bad ways. That Hispanic communities would spring up was probably natural enough. But by the same token, that an element of prejudice was present in that would be probable. At any rate, all the towns on the Union Pacific had Hispanic neighborhoods, and many still do. Cheyenne, for example, has South Cheyenne, a neighborhood that lies to the south of the Union Pacific and features a very Spanish-influenced church architecturally, as well as a Mexican restaurant reputed to be one of the town's best.

Laramie, generally thought of as the home of the University of Wyoming, likewise has a Hispanic-influenced neighborhood, reflecting the large Hispanic community that worked in the very large rail yard in Laramie. Not surprisingly, perhaps, Laramie has an excellent Mexican restaurant in West Laramie, the Hispanic part of town, and another just off the Union Pacific rail line. Hispanics are a significant portion of the Catholic community in the town as well.

Like Laramie and Cheyenne, Rawlins has a Hispanic neighborhood associated with the Union Pacific. And as with Laramie and Cheyenne, Carbon County has seen the culture reflected in culinary offerings. Su Casa in Sinclair and Rose's Lariat in Rawlins are contenders for the best Mexican restaurants in the state, and even though they are only seven miles apart, each has a fiercely loyal clientele. All the way across the state, however, the farming and railroad town of Lingle has Lira's, which others argue is the best. Guernsey, on the Burlington Northern line, had Otero's Kitchen, which others maintained was the best. I've eaten at every one mentioned here, and they're all great.

To mention all these restaurants in this context may seem shallow, but it's a reflection of a long-lasting and vibrant culture. Mexican restaurants owned by Hispanic families only preserve for years and years, rather than becoming something like Taco Bell, if there's a vibrant Hispanic community that has become part of the local community. So the culinary reflection indicates something deeper than just a regional taste for Mexican food. Rather, it is indicative of the fact that all these railroad towns had, and still have, vibrant Hispanic communities.

This has reflected itself over the years, additionally, through the Catholic churches in these towns. In no area of Wyoming is any one parish made up of a majority Hispanic population, but in those towns where there is a significant Hispanic population, it has reflected itself in some way. Those towns with significant Hispanic populations have seen it reflected, for example, in the celebration of Our Lady of Guadalupe events. When I lived in Laramie in the 1980s, for example, St. Lawrence O'Toole's parish crowned a young couple as king and queen of the event and had a major celebration in church, complete with a brass and guitar band. St. Anthony's Church in Casper has sometimes seen similar, if less extensive, events.

Of course, with a long presence in the state, it's not surprising that the Hispanic community has members in every walk of life and profession. Prominent educators, lawyers and physicians have come from within the community and contributed to the state.

Unlike the story of the Irish in Wyoming, this story really cannot be completely written at this time, as Wyoming's towns and industries have seen new Hispanic immigrants in recent years. Receiving an influx of workers during boom times, to see an outward migration thereafter, is part of Wyoming's economic history, so how the current new residents will impact the state is really not known. However, heavy industry, including the oil and gas industry, has employed a lot of migrant workers in recent years. As has been the case for generations, service industries have as well so that towns like Jackson, which at one time had fairly small Hispanic communities, now have very prominent ones. So this story is incomplete. But like the story of the Irish, it is one that goes back to the state's very beginnings.

1891 Green River is incorporated.

1908 The first meeting of the Wyoming Farmers Congress takes place in Cheyenne.

May 6

1889 Casper is incorporated.

Casper in 1890. *Courtesy of Wyoming State Archives, Department of State Parks and Cultural Resources.*

1898 Elmer Lovejoy demonstrates his automobile in Laramie.

May 7

1868 A treaty is signed with the Crows at Fort Laramie.

1898 Elmer Lovejoy demonstrates his automobile in Laramie.

May 8

1860 Captain W.F. Reynolds's expedition leaves Deer Creek. Its intention was to follow the Wind River to its headwaters and then cross a divide to the headwaters of the Yellowstone.

1868 Union Pacific completes tracks to Fort Saunders.

1938 Alcova Dam on the North Platte is completed.

Alcova Reservoir as viewed from the top of Alcova Dam. The reservoir is a favorite for area boaters and water sports enthusiasts. *Photograph by the author.*

1946 Wyoming Game & Fish districts are created.

May 9

1868 Union Pacific completes tracks to Laramie.

1886 The legislature approves the creation of a mental hospital in Evanston.

1911 Susan Wissler, elected mayor of Dayton, becomes the first woman to be elected as a mayor in Wyoming. She lived a long but hard life, having come to Wyoming with her husband and children in 1900. Her husband died in 1906, and she did not remarry. She was a milliner by trade but was employed in Dayton as a schoolteacher. In her later years, she was in constant ill health, but she lived to age eighty-five. She served as mayor for two years.

May 10

1868 The first train enters Laramie.

1910 Powell is incorporated.

1944 Tom Bell, the founder of the Wyoming Outdoor Council, is wounded in action in a B-24 mission over Austria. He would lose his right eye as a result of his injuries.

May 11

1950 The remains of Big Nose George Parrott are found by workmen working on the Rawlins National Bank. Parrott's remains had been given to Dr. John Osborne, who was later elected governor, for study. Osborne stored the body in a salted whiskey barrel and eventually buried the whiskey barrel in the yard behind his office. The entire story of the treatment of Parrott's body following his execution is shocking by modern standards, including the means of finally laying him to rest until this date in 1950.

May 12

1865 Colonel Thomas Moonlight's expedition of the recently arrived Eleventh Kansas Cavalry reaches the Wind River in Wyoming but fails to encounter the Cheyenne, who were raiding west of Fort Laramie, for whom he was searching.

1920 The Wyoming National Guard is reconstituted as the First Regiment, Wyoming Cavalry.

May 13

1907 The U.S. Supreme Court rules that a popular vote in 1892 concerning the location of the "Agricultural College of Wyoming" was advisory, thereby keeping the University of Wyoming in Laramie rather than moving it to Lander.

1912 The first political conventions in the state to nominate presidential electors take place in Cheyenne.

1919 Movie star and recent veteran of the U.S. Army (artillery officer in World War I) Tim McCoy becomes the adjutant general for the Wyoming National Guard. In that capacity, he received a brevet rank of brigadier general at age twenty-eight. He retained that position until 1921, when, I believe, it reverted to extraordinarily long-serving General Esmay, who had held it prior to World War I, with some interruption.

McCoy was also ranching in Wyoming during this time frame. He ran for the U.S. Senate in Wyoming in 1942 but lost, rejoining the army as an officer the day after his defeat. He served in the U.S. Army Air Corps in Europe during World War II and reportedly never returned to Wyoming after the war.

Evincing a surprising lack of sentiment about horses for a film star of this early era, McCoy is known to have remarked that he was not sentimental about horses: "If you want to know the truth—horses are dumb."

May 14

1890 Weston County elects its first county officers.

May 15

1888 Voters choose Douglas as the county seat of Converse County.

1889 The state mental hospital opens in Evanston.

1930 Ellen Church, the first airline stewardess, goes on duty aboard a United Airlines flight from San Francisco to Cheyenne.

May 16

1986 The Cokeville Elementary School crisis occurs when David Young and Doris Young take 167 hostages—150 children and 17 adults, one being an unlucky UPS driver—at the school by bringing in a bomb to which the couple attached themselves with a lanyard. David Young had been the town marshal but had been fired for his odd, erratic behavior. Doris Young had been a café worker in the town whom he had met while living there. David claimed to be acting as a revolutionary, but part of his demands included $300 million. Doris accidentally detonated the bomb while her deluded husband was using a restroom. He returned and murdered her and then killed himself after wounding a teacher. All the hostages survived, many leaving the classroom through the windows after the blast. The incident is extremely unusual in that it was associated with a very large number of reports of the presence of angels seconds prior to the blast, who, according to those present, directed everyone to the far side of the room near the windows.

May 17

1902 Rock Springs hits its record high temperature, 112 degrees Fahrenheit.

1921 Laramie's Elmer Lovejoy patents a Trackage for Ceiling Type of Doors with Door-Openers (Patent No. 1,378,123).

1928 Mother Featherlegs Monument is dedicated in Lusk.

May 18

1868 Fort Morgan, Colorado, is abandoned. Its garrison is transferred to Fort Laramie.

1874 Captain F. Van Vliet, Company C, Third Cavalry, who was at that time stationed at Fort Fetterman, Wyoming, writes to the adjutant general requesting that his company be transferred because there was "no opportunity for procuring fresh vegetables, and gardens are a failure. There is no female society for enlisted men...the enlisted men of the company are leaving very much dissatisfied, as they look upon being held so long at this post as an unmerited punishment...whenever men get to the railroad there are some desertions caused by dread of returning to this post." Fort Fetterman was a hardship post and had the highest rate of insanity in the frontier army.

1882 Fort Sanders, near Laramie, is abandoned. By this point in time, those forts built principally to defend the Union Pacific Railroad were no longer needed for multiple reasons, one being the ability of the railroad to transport troops.

1887 The cornerstone is laid for the state capitol.

The state capitol in the 1950s. *Photograph by Thomas L. Holscher.*

1898 Wyoming volunteers for service in the Philippines board a train for San Francisco.

1898 Troop L, Second U.S. Volunteer Cavalry, made up of men from around Evanston and Kemmerer, is mustered into the United States service.

May 19

1848 Mexico ratifies the Treaty of Guadalupe Hidalgo acknowledging the acquisition by the United States of Texas and New Mexico, which includes a small portion of Wyoming, via Texas.

1846 President Polk approves an act that provides for a line of military posts along the Oregon Trail. In some ways, this has to be regarded as a major development in the history of the United States and the U.S. Army, as the expansion of the army onto the western frontier dominated much of its character for the next century, even continuing to have an influence into its nature well after the frontier had closed.

1866 Colonel Carrington leaves Fort Kearny for Fort Laramie, where he receives instructions from General Pope to name two new outposts along Bozeman Road Fort Philip Kearny and Fort C.F. Smith. The widely spaced forts were to form more northerly bastions to guard the Bozeman Trail, with the southernmost post, Fort Reno, having already been established during the Civil War by Patrick Connor. Carrington was one of a group of officers who remained in the army following the Civil War when Congress established the policy of making room for some wartime officers who had not come from prewar military service or West Point. Alfred Terry was another, with both men having been lawyers prior to the Civil War.

1902 The first Carnegie Library in the United States, the Laramie County Library, opens.

1938 Niobrara County, Wyoming, becomes the first county in the United States to have all its mail for a day delivered via airmail.

May 20

1862 Congress passes the Homestead Act. As surprising as it is now to think of it, the Homestead Act remained in force until 1932 in the lower forty-eight. The last patents were taken out under the various acts in the 1950s, although entries could still be made in Alaska up until some date in the 1950s. Homesteading remained quite active in the 1919 to 1932 period, as there were efforts to encourage veterans to homestead following World War I, and there was a lot of desperate homesteading in the 1929 to 1932 time frame. A Wyoming Supreme Court decision on a land contest from that period actually noted that no decision could be reached, as homesteading was carving up the contested lands so fast that the decision would be obsolete by the time it was rendered. The repeal of the act in 1932 was followed by the failure of many of the late smaller homesteads and a reversal of the trend. The federal government reacquired many of the late homesteads by default and actually purchased a large number of them in the Thunder Basin region of Wyoming, as it was so clear that they would fail in the droughts of the '30s.

Following up a bit, it's interesting to note that there were more homesteads taken out under the various Homestead Acts in the twentieth century than there were in the nineteenth. The 1914 to 1919 period saw a huge boom in homesteading.

One of the most interesting things about the act was said to me by the grandson of Russian immigrants who had homesteaded outside Cheyenne, that simply being that "it was a good deal for poor people." I suppose that is true.

1865 Sioux and Cheyenne attack Three Crossings, Wyoming, which results in the death of one of the attacking warriors.

1879 Peder Bergersan of Cheyenne issues a patent for an improvement in magazine firearms.

May 21

1865 Sioux and Cheyenne attack a three-man party of troopers of the Eleventh Kansas led by Second Lieutenant W.B. Godfrey three miles above Deer Creek Station, Wyoming, while another party of fifty warriors attacks the six-man Eleventh Kansas contingent in a nearby camp. A party of two hundred Indians drove the horse herd off at Deer Creek Station and was given chase by a thirty-man contingent of troopers, led by Colonel Plumb, who were not able to ford the North Platte due to the spring runoff.

1888 Converse County is organized.

1898 Wyoming volunteers for the war in the Philippines arrive in San Francisco and Camp Merritt.

1934 Company No. 844 of the Civilian Conservation Corps arrives at Guernsey State Park to begin work on construction projects. Ultimately, they would go on to build the officers' quarters at Camp Guernsey, the new National Guard facility that replaced Pole Mountain as the training range for the Wyoming National Guard. Camp Guernsey received only one or two annual training cycles prior to World War II but has remained the training range since that time. Now much expanded, it is also used by the U.S. Army and the United States Marine Corps for training missions.

After World War II, the guard would install Quonset huts for the enlisted barracks, but I believe those were recently replaced.

May 22

1891 The Lincoln Land Company purchases the land on which Moorcroft would be built.

1902 Medicine Bow Forest Reserve is established by President Theodore Roosevelt.

1978 The Virginian Hotel and the Riverton Railroad Depot are added to the National Register of Historic Places.

The Virginian Hotel. *Photograph by the author.*

1991 The 1022nd Medical Company returns to state control.

May 23

1865 Sioux and Cheyenne raiders return to Deer Creek Station and try again.

1898 Troop C of the Second U.S. Volunteer Cavalry, "Torrey's Rough Riders," recruited in the vicinity of Laramie, musters in at Fort D.A. Russell. Troop E was also mustered in and had been recruited in the counties of Sheridan, Crook and Weston.

1942 The site for the Heart Mountain, Wyoming internment camp is selected.

May 24

1865 Three Cheyenne or Sioux warriors attempt to drive off the horses at Sweetwater Station, Wyoming. One of them was killed in the process.

1869 John Wesley Powell's expedition leaves Green River.

May 25

1865 An Indian raid on the stage station on Green River drives off stock.

1909 The Reclamation Service sells lots in Powell, founding the town.

1971 Major William E. Adams, U.S. Army, performs the actions that result in his being awarded the Congressional Medal of Honor, but he loses his life in the process. He was a member of the A/227th Assault Helicopter Company, 52nd Aviation Battalion, 1st Aviation Brigade. He entered the service from Kansas City, Missouri, but was born in Casper on June 16, 1939. His citation reads as follows:

> *Maj. Adams distinguished himself on 25 May 1971 while serving as a helicopter pilot in Kontum Province in the Republic of Vietnam. On that date, Maj. Adams volunteered to fly a lightly armed helicopter in an attempt to evacuate 3 seriously wounded soldiers from a small fire base which was under attack by a large enemy force. He made the decision with full knowledge that numerous antiaircraft weapons were positioned around the base and that the clear weather would afford the enemy gunners unobstructed view of all routes into the base. As he approached the base, the*

enemy gunners opened fire with heavy machine guns, rocket-propelled grenades and small arms. Undaunted by the fusillade, he continued his approach determined to accomplish the mission. Displaying tremendous courage under fire, he calmly directed the attacks of supporting gunships while maintaining absolute control of the helicopter he was flying. He landed the aircraft at the fire base despite the ever-increasing enemy fire and calmly waited until the wounded soldiers were placed on board. As his aircraft departed from the fire base, it was struck and seriously damaged by enemy anti-aircraft fire and began descending. Flying with exceptional skill, he immediately regained control of the crippled aircraft and attempted a controlled landing. Despite his valiant efforts, the helicopter exploded, overturned, and plummeted to earth amid the hail of enemy fire. Maj. Adams' conspicuous gallantry, intrepidity, and humanitarian regard for his fellow man were in keeping with the most cherished traditions of the military service and reflected utmost credit on him and the U.S. Army.

1975 Midwest is incorporated.

May 26

1864 Montana Territory is established. Wyoming was part of it at the time.

1882 The Cheyenne Opera House opens.

1882 Frank Collins Emerson is born in Saginaw, Michigan. He became the state engineer in 1919 and governor in 1927. He would die in office in 1931.

1896 The graves at the military cemetery located at LaBonte PO are relocated to Fort McPherson, Nebraska.

1921 Eddie Rickenbacker crashes a mail plane near Cheyenne.

2001 Laurence Rockefeller donates his Wyoming ranch to the national parks system.

May 27

1876 The Powder River Expedition leaves Fort Fetterman.

1893 The first electric lights in Sheridan are turned on at the Sheridan Inn.

The Sheridan Inn. *Photograph by the author.*

1898 Troop F, Second U.S. Volunteer Cavalry, coming from Rock Springs, Green River and Cheyenne, is mustered in at Fort Russell.

1944 Roy Rogers buys a horse to act as a Trigger stand-in in Lusk, Wyoming.

May 28

1865 Cheyenne and/or Sioux attack Elkhorn Station, Wyoming, with inconclusive results. They also attacked Sweetwater Station, Wyoming, and took four horses and two mules and Pole Creek Station, Wyoming.

1869 Territorial governor Campbell issues an order for a census of Wyoming Territory.

1902 Owen Wister's classic novel *The Virginian* is published.

May 29

1890 Wyoming's first federally recognized National Guard unit is formed, Company A, First Wyoming Regiment, the Laramie Grays. The Laramie Grays were a short-lived cavalry unit. In spite of the absolute dependence on the horse for the economy of the region, Wyoming National Guard units were generally infantry and then artillery up until after World War I.

1903 President Theodore Roosevelt makes a whistle stop in Evanston.

1904 A Natrona County boy is shot while herding sheep at Alkali Gulch.

May 30

1834 William Sublette and William Anderson arrive at "Laramee's Fork," named for the late Jacque LaRamie, a trapper who had been killed there. The next day, they laid the foundation logs for Fort William, which would become Fort Laramie.

1854 The territories of Nebraska and Kansas are established. Wyoming east of the Rocky Mountains was included in the Nebraska Territory.

1862 Companies A, B, C and D of the First Battalion of the Sixth Ohio Volunteer Cavalry arrive at Fort Laramie.

1865 Cheyenne and/or Sioux attack Three Crossings Station.

1871 Wyoming Stock Growers Association, which would have an enormous impact on Wyoming's history, is formed.

1903 Theodore Roosevelt visits Cheyenne and Laramie. He stopped first in Laramie, where he delivered a speech at Old Main. Invited by Rough Rider veterans to ride to the next stop, Cheyenne, he did so.

A stereograph of Theodore Roosevelt in Wyoming. *Library of Congress.*

1904 Sheep rancher Lincoln Morrison is shot in an ambush near Kirby Creek, Hot Springs County. He survived. His mother, Lucy Morrison Moore, the "Sheep Queen," offered a $3,500 reward, but the attempted murderer was not discovered.

1908 An Evanston-to-Denver horse race commences.

May 31

1834 Sublette and Campbell start constructing Fort William, which would later become Fort Laramie.

1903 Theodore Roosevelt attends church in Cheyenne (it was a Sunday) and lunches with Joseph Carey.

JUNE IN WYOMING

June sees the full commencement of summer in Wyoming. The month may have the best weather of the year, although the occasional snowstorm can still occur and does every year to some extent in the high country. As school gets out, Wyomingites turn to the lakes, rivers and mountains for recreation.

The month has always been a big one for stockmen as well, who have long driven their herds to the high country, an annual ritual that still occurs every June.

Trailing cattle.
Photograph by Marcus Holscher.

June 1

1865 Sioux and/or Cheyenne attempt to drive stock off Sweetwater Station. They burned Rocky Ridge Station that night but dispersed when the blackpowder stores exploded. The five enlisted men of the Eleventh Ohio stationed there took refuge in the well.

1909 Pathfinder Dam is completed.

1933 The first Wyoming Highway Patrolman assumes duties. The WYHP grew out of Prohibition enforcement.

June 2

1865 Sioux and Cheyenne attack Platte Bridge Station. The Indians approached the station and fired on it, and the men of the Eleventh Ohio gave chase. They ran into trouble when the Indian band they were chasing, only ten men, turned out to be a lure and they were ambushed. Fortunately for them, at that moment a detachment from the Eleventh Kansas arrived, and a running fight ensued. Two troopers and one Indian were killed.

1899 The Wild Bunch robs the Union Pacific Overland Flyer No. 1 near Wilcox, taking between $30,000 and $60,000. This robbery is famous in part for the large amount taken but also for the destruction of a rail car by explosives that were used to open a safe. This is depicted in the film *Butch Cassidy and the Sundance Kid*.

1924 Congress passes the Indian Citizenship Act, conferring citizenship on all Native Americans born within the territorial limits of the country.

1945 Fort F.E. Warren is made a redeployment center for quartermaster and transportation corps troops, a rather surprising thing considering how late in World War II this was.

June 3

1862 Sixth Ohio Cavalry regimental commander Lieutenant Colonel William O. Collins receives orders to take three companies to South Pass to protect the employees and property of the Overland Mail Company and the Pacific Telegraph.

1926 A training camp for the National Guard at Pole Mountain is approved.

1948 Thirty-eight contestants enter a horse race between Sheridan, Wyoming, and Billings, Montana, 137 miles. The state had a culture of long-distance horse races at the time.

June 4

1922 Legendary Wyoming oilman and philanthropist Fred Goldstein marries Ida Goldberg in Denver. Goldstein is an example of how a lack of education was not a bar to success in his era. He attended school only through grade eight before going to work in American Pipe & Supply, his father's company, in Denver. This would lead to a career that would make him enormously financially successful and would also have a dramatic impact on Casper, where he ultimately relocated to direct the company's activities.

June 5

1853 The first hostile encounter between the Sioux and the U.S. Army occurs near Fort Laramie.

1889 Wyoming appoints a resident to the United States Military Academy for the first time.

1922 The United States Supreme Court rules in Wyoming's favor in *Wyoming v. Colorado*, thereby ruling in favor of the state's prior appropriation of the Laramie River.

June 6

1892 Information is filed in *State of Wyoming v. Alexander Adamson, et al. Murder in the First Degree*, charging Alexander Adamson, William E. Guthrie, William Armstrong and J.A. Garrett with the murder of Rueben "Nick" Ray during the Johnson County War. This was a criminal charge filed in Johnson County as opposed to Laramie County.

1908 A man from Cody is the co-winner of the Evanston, Wyoming–Denver horse race, one of the long-distance horse races that were common in Wyoming at the time.

1912 President Taft signs the Homestead Act of 1912, which reduces the period to "prove up" from five years to three. This was unknowingly on the eve of a major boom in homesteading, as World War I would create a huge demand for wheat for export, followed by the largest number of homestead filings in American history as would-be wheat farmers attempted to gain land for the endeavor.

1915 British commissioners begin to purchase remounts in Wyoming. The purchase of horses for British service in World War I created a boom in horse ranching that would continue to be fueled by both British and American service purchases throughout the war but would be followed by a horse ranching crash after the war.

June 7

1869 Fort Bridger Treaty is signed between the United States and Shoshone tribes.

June 8

1888 John Merritt and C.W. Eads establish the town of Casper. Their initial site would be at the present-day intersection of McKinley and A Streets and anticipated the arrival of the Fremont, Elkhorn and Missouri Valley Railroad (Burlington Northern Railroad) the following week. Present-day Eadsville, once an independent town but now part of Casper, is named after Eads.

1974 Suddenly a pop icon years after his death due to the movie *Jeremiah Johnson*, Mexican War veteran, frontiersman, trapper and former Cody sheriff John "Liver Eating" Johnston is reinterred at the Cody Cemetery. Robert Redford, who played him in the film, was on hand.

June 9

1870 President Grant meets with Sioux chief Red Cloud. Red Cloud is often noted as the only Plains Indian leader who won a war against the United States, that being Red Cloud's War in Wyoming. Following his trip east, Red Cloud realized that the population of the United States made any war against it futile and worked for peaceful positions for his tribe.

Red Cloud. *Library of Congress.*

June 10

1858 The U.S. Army takes control of Fort Bridger.

1888 A baseball game between Fort McKinney and the town team for Buffalo results in a Fort McKinney win. Baseball was well on its way to becoming the national sport at the time.

1890 Fort Laramie's grounds and associated timber reserves are transferred to the Department of the Interior.

June 11

1865 A party of Sioux is force-marched from Fort Laramie to Fort Kearney, Nebraska.

1898 Recruiting begins for the Alger Light Artillery of Cheyenne, which would enter federal service as Battery A, Wyoming Light Artillery.

1912 The Franco-Wyoming Oil Company opens a refinery in Casper near the present intersection of Beverly and Fourth Streets. This was Casper's second refinery (the first had closed), but there would be an additional one by the end of the year.

June 12

1847 Mormon migrants in Brigham Young's wagon train reach the Platte River near the present location of Casper.

1863 The first newspaper in Wyoming is published in Fort Bridger.

1867 The Second Cavalry sustains a loss when a trooper is killed by Indians at Fort Phil Kearny.

1867 Negotiations with Man Afraid of His Horses at Fort Laramie break down over his request for ammunition.

1880 The remaining portions of Crow territory in Wyoming are ceded to the United States.

1890 The brewery in Laramie sells its first beer. Up until Prohibition, small local breweries were extremely common in the United States.

1920 The 1ˢᵗ Regiment, Wyoming Cavalry, National Guard, is organized. It would become the 115ᵗʰ Cavalry Regiment in 1922.

Contrary to what many might expect, cavalry units in the National Guard were greatly expanded following World War I as the National Guard became more closely aligned with the overall needs of the U.S. Army.

June 13

1866 Negotiations between U.S. and Sioux representatives take place at Fort Phil Kearny.

1889 Rawlins receives two feet of snow.

1979 The Sioux are awarded $105 million for the U.S. seizure of the Black Hills in the nineteenth century.

June 14 — Flag Day

1845 Five companies of the First Dragoons arrive at Fort Laramie.

June 15

1846 Representatives of Great Britain and the United States sign the Oregon Treaty, which settles a long-standing dispute with Britain over who controlled the Oregon Territory, including that portion of Wyoming west of the Rocky Mountains.

1853 A skirmish occurs at Fort Laramie over the attempted arrest of a Sioux who had fired a shot at a soldier as part of an argument. The skirmish resulted in the death of three Indians, but a disaster was averted as Indian leaders convinced their fellows not to advance or further engage in spite of the fact that they grossly outnumbered the soldiers present.

1888 The first train arrives in Casper. Note, from earlier entries, that Casper had existed for about a week at the time.

1898 The Alger Light Artillery of Cheyenne enters U.S. service as Battery A, Wyoming Light Artillery.

1935 Congress passes the act allowing for the expansion of the National Elk Refuge.

June 16

1971 Bill Briggs descends the Grand Tetons on skis, the first person to do so.

June 17

1849 The United States flag rises at Fort Laramie, now a military post.

1866 Colonel Henry B. Carrington's column leaves Fort Laramie and starts up the Bozeman Trail. The command arrived at Fort Reno on June 28.

1904 Harry Hudson and John H. Henderlite fight at their sheep camp in the Big Horns, and Hudson kills Henderlite. Hudson claimed self-defense and asserted that Henderlite came at him with a knife. He was arrested but let go for lack of evidence. Henderlite was buried on location.

A lonely sheepherder's grave. *Photograph by the author.*

1916 The Wyoming National Guard is mobilized and federalized for Mexican border service. On this same eventful day, additional American troops under the command of General Pershing enter Mexico in an effort to track down Pancho Villa.

1921 Lightning strikes and ignites several oil tanks owned by Midwest Oil Company outside Casper. The fire that resulted burned for sixty hours and consumed more than a half million gallons of oil. It was a major disaster at the time.

June 18

1893 Sheridan Inn opens.

1907 The first train arrives in Centennial, where today there is a train museum.

June 19

1886 The cornerstone is laid at the Union Pacific Depot in Cheyenne.

1916 Orders are received in Wyoming from the War Department to mobilize two battalions of the Wyoming National Guard for border service. On September 28, the troops departed for the Mexican border.

1954 Wyoming senator Lester C. Hunt commits suicide. The tragedy came about after his twenty-year-old son was arrested for soliciting services from a male prostitute. Hunt's son was not prosecuted, and the matter was quietly dropped, but the news was broken by the *Washington Times-Herald*, and Hunt was threatened early on with political opposition based on the event. He was an opponent of Senator Joseph McCarthy, and there was some suspicion that a comment from McCarthy also vaguely referred to his son's conduct.

June 20

1865 Arapahos attack the eight men of Company G, Eleventh Ohio Cavalry, and the civilian telegraph operator ten miles east of Sweetwater Station, Wyoming, while they are repairing the telegraph line. The cavalrymen were grossly outnumbered in the assault. Three Arapahos and the telegraph operator were killed in the engagement.

1868 Fort Fred Steele is established.

1912 The State Training School opens in Lander.

1912 An explosion at the No. 4 Mine near Kemmerer kills six miners.

1954 Drew Pearson publishes an account of Senator Lester Hunt's suicide, in which he notes that the Democratic senator had related to Pearson how Republican senators had threatened to seek the prosecution of his son if he did not resign from the Senate but otherwise describes the motivations for his suicide as complex. See June 19 entry for more on this story.

June 21

Today is the Summer Solstice and the first day of summer, except in leap years, when it occurs the day prior.

1880 Harry Yount receives word of his appointment as a wildlife officer for Yellowstone National Park, the first person to occupy such a position. He occupied it for only about a year but is regarded as a pioneer in the field.

1923 The Jordan Automobile Company, which would not survive the Great Depression, introduces a new style of advertising based on image rather than direct citations to the qualities of its product, thereby revolutionizing advertising.

Edward Jordan, the founder of the company, had been an advertising man. The advertising campaign was inspired by Jordan actually seeing a young woman riding near the Union Pacific rail line near Laramie while he was a passenger in the train.

1963 The Wyoming Air National Guard's 187th Aeromedical Transport Squadron receives C-121 Super Constellation aircraft.

Somewhere West of Laramie

SOMEWHERE west of Laramie there's a broncho-busting, steer-roping girl who knows what I'm talking about. She can tell what a sassy pony, that's a cross between greased lightning and the place where it hits, can do with eleven hundred pounds of steel and action when he's going high, wide and handsome.

The truth is—the Jordan Playboy was built for her.

JORDAN

JORDAN MOTOR CAR COMPANY, Inc., Cleveland, Ohio

The Jordan Automobile Company would not endure the Great Depression, but its advertising style would. The advertising copy here enigmatically read: "SOMEWHERE west of Laramie there's a bronco-busting, steer roping girl who knows what I'm talking about. She can tell what a sassy pony, that's a cross between greased lighting and the place where it hits, can do with eleven hundred pounds of steel and action when he's going high, wide and handsome. The truth is—the Playboy was built for her. Built for the lass whose face is brown with the sun when the day is done of revel and romp and race. She loves the cross of the wild and the tame. There's a savor of links about that car—of laughter and lilt and light—a hint of old loves—and saddle and quirt. It's a brawny thing—yet a graceful thing for the sweep o' the Avenue. Step into the Playboy when the hour grows dull with things gone dead and stale. Then start for the land of real living with the spirit of the lass who rides, lean and rangy, into the red horizon of a Wyoming twilight." *Library of Congress.*

June 22

1898 The Second U.S. Volunteer Cavalry, "Torrey's Rough Riders," leaves Cheyenne by rail for Camp Cuba Libre in Jacksonville, Florida.

Colonel J.L. Torrey at Fort D.A. Russell. *Courtesy of Wyoming State Archives, Department of State Parks and Cultural Resources.*

1947 Heavy snowfall threatens to cancel a Gillette-to-Douglas horse race.

June 23

1810 John Jacob Astor forms the Pacific Fur Company.

1923 President Harding crosses Wyoming by train.

June 24

1876 Albert Curtis is killed by A.W. Chandler on the Little Laramie River for sheep trespassing. This 1876 killing is a surprisingly early incident in what would come to be increasing violence between sheepmen and cattlemen. Curtis's father was a judge in Ohio.

1898 Battery A, Wyoming Light Artillery, leaves for San Francisco for deployment to the Philippines.

1939 The first performance of the Cody night rodeo occurs.

June 25

1868 President Andrew Johnson approves the act of Congress providing for the organization of a temporary government for the Territory of Wyoming.

1870 The first lots go on sale at the site of Evanston.

June 26

1865 Company I, Eleventh Kansas, is attacked by a large party of Cheyenne/Sioux while repairing a telegraph line near Red Buttes, Wyoming. The men expended between thirty-six and sixty rounds of ammunition each, taking two wounded in a hard-fought action that took them back to Platte Bridge Station, a distance of six miles.

1909 Medicine Bow becomes an incorporated town.

June 27

1898 The First Wyoming Volunteer Infantry, part of the Third Philippine Expedition, is with the expedition when it leaves for the Philippines starting on this day. The process would take through the twenty-ninth.

June 28

1869 Camp Augur is established by the army near the current town of Lander. In 1870, the post was renamed Camp Brown. On the same day, the Wind River Indian Reservation was established near the present site of Lander. In 1871, Camp Brown was moved to the current site of Fort Washakie on the reservation.

1919 Van Tassel, in Niobrara County, receives the first charter for an American Legion post in the United States. The American Legion only recently had been formed in Paris by veterans of World War I. The post in the now long-gone town was named for Ferdinand Branstetter, a resident of the town who was killed in World War I.

1934 The Taylor Grazing Act passes Congress. This major act completely re-formed how the federal domain was held, ending homesteading and initiating a lease system for the remaining federal domain.

1937 The first technical climbing ascent of Devil's Tower is accomplished by Fritz Wiessner, Lawrence Coveney and William P. House.

June 29

1923 The Ku Klux Klan marches in Glenrock. This seems like an extremely surprising item today, but the early 1920s were the high-water mark of the KKK, which had been revived following the success of D.W. Griffith's film *Birth of a Nation*, which took a very Confederate view of the Civil War and Reconstruction and would be regarded as racist today. The KKK and other racist and nativist organizations were surprisingly present in some western states at this time, but they were never strong in Wyoming.

June 30

1868 Fort Fred Steele is established where the Union Pacific Railroad crosses the North Platte River.

1903 A deadly mine explosion in Hanna kills 169 miners.

The mine memorial in Hanna. The bodies of 201 miners were not recovered from the 1903 and 1908 disasters and remain in the collapsed mine. *Photograph by the author.*

2009 In a move that was controversial among alumni of the University of Wyoming's Geology Department, the Geological Museum is closed due to state budget cuts.

JULY IN WYOMING

July is one of the hottest months of the year in Wyoming, followed by August, and is a month that may begin to cause concerns for the water supply for farms and ranches for the rest of the summer. Historically, it's also a month that saw a great deal of Indian Wars activity in the state, which brings us to a group of people we have not yet addressed: Native Americans.

Sidebar:
Native Americans in Wyoming

It's common to see terms such as "Plains Indians" and the like to describe the native inhabitants of any one region of the upper West, but the fact of the matter is that Indian tribes represent a group of ethnicities rather than one single one. Still, as an introduction, it makes sense to at least handle the topic collectively to get it rolling.

In the popular imagination, Pre-Colombian North America was populated by rather fixed Indian populations. In reality, however, this was far from true, and this was particularly untrue in the arid West. Native populations were not only aboriginal, but also they were in a near constant state of migration, albeit slow migration, prior to their contact with European Americans and even after it. We know, for example, that both the Navajos and the Apaches are Athabascan peoples whose nearest ethnic relatives live in the Canadian far north. The Navajos first and the Apaches after them started migrating south at some point for reasons not known, and when the Spanish first came into contact with them, they were still on their way south. Their cultural consciousness still retained memories of great white bears and fields of migrating birds, things their ancestors had observed in the far North decades and decades prior but not so long ago that the memory was not retained. And so, too, with many other Indian cultures.

For the most part, the history of Indians in the West begins with their first contact with Europeans operating out of the United States, Mexico or Quebec. What occurred prior to that is a bit murky. We know that Wyoming, in ancient times, had populations of natives who built pit houses, a practice not engaged in by any of the later tribes. These houses might very well have been constructed by the ancestors of a people who had moved far to the south by the time the Corps of Discovery made the first U.S. tour of the area. That early history is important, however, in that these people left some sort of a record of their presence. Seemingly living in a somewhat wetter era, they lived in a less nomadic manner than their later ancestors and had seasonal fixed dwellings. Theories exist as to who they may have been, and we don't really have a very solid idea of what people or peoples they were other than that they were there. They also seem to have been the first people to leave a record in stone, such as with the Medicine Wheel, with such structures remaining in use by later peoples who perhaps conceived of them differently. Research goes on, and perhaps someday we'll know a great deal more than we currently do.

More recently, we know that Wyoming was the home of certain tribes in the eighteenth century who remained in the nineteenth century. The Shoshone, a people speaking an Utzo-Aztec language, was one of those groups and perhaps the most dominant.

The Shoshone had a long and significant presence in the state. They still do, as they are one of the two tribes that have as their home the Wind River Indian Reservation. The eastern Shoshone are the branch of the tribe who inhabited Wyoming, with various other branches at once inhabiting a vast tract of land stretching all the way to California. Sometimes called the "Snake" Indians by other peoples, in the nineteenth century they came under pressure from invading bands of other native groups and, perhaps for this reason, were generally allied in Wyoming to the United States. The Wind River Reservation, a large reservation in central Wyoming, was originally set aside for the Shoshone. The Shoshone contributed famously to the history of the United States in the form of Sacajawea, who was Shoshone, but also in the form of native allies of the United States in the Indian Wars of the late nineteenth century. A branch of the Shoshone called the Mountain Shoshone or the "Sheepeaters" remained fully aboriginal until very late in the nineteenth century, when they were finally induced to join their relatives on the Wind River Reservation. The most well-known chief of the nineteenth-century Shoshone was Chief Washakie, who, in statutory form, represents Wyoming in Washington, D.C. Washakie, who was instrumental in easing the tribe into the traumatic changes of the nineteenth century, may have lived to be 102 years old.

The Crows, or Absarokas, likewise had a long history in the state. The Crows speak a Siouan language and were a significant Plains people whose range stretched far into Wyoming when European Americans first entered the state. The Crows and Shoshone fought each other prior to European American contact, but they were both allies of the United States in the Indian Wars of the 1860s and 1870s, as they attempted to arrest the progress of the Sioux and Cheyenne in entering the state. Unlike the Shoshone, the Crows do not have a reservation in Wyoming, but they still have some presence, and the major Crow reservation is located just over the Montana border. They leave a record of their nearby presence in the part of a mountain range, the Absarokas, which has recently become well known due to the fictional Absaroka County featured in the television series *Longmire*.

The Sioux, a collection of closely related people, and the Cheyenne, a group that was allied to them, likewise had a major role in the state. Neither group had a long history in the state or perhaps even any history when European Americans first entered Wyoming. The Sioux and the Cheyenne were, rather, invaders, and highly successful ones at that. Interestingly, their alliance was one that overcame an ethnic divide between the people, as the Cheyenne spoke an Algonquian language, not a Siouan one. The Cheyenne, for their part, were a stunningly wide-ranging people whose presence stretched northward into Montana and southward down to Oklahoma. As with the Crows, neither the Sioux nor the Cheyenne have reservations in Wyoming, but they do have ones nearby, with there being a Sioux reservation in South Dakota and a Cheyenne reservation in Montana. Both groups figured spectacularly in the Plains Indians Wars and were really the main contestants for the land against the United States. Nearly all of the Indian Wars battles mentioned in this book were fought by the Sioux and the Cheyenne, often allied in the same battle, against the United States. Red Cloud, a Sioux leader, is credited with being the only Plains Indian leader to have defeated the United States at war, with the result of Red Cloud's War being the abandonment of the Powder River Basin and the Bozeman Trail, together with the forts protecting it. The loss would be a temporary one for the United States, but still, it was an Indian victory.

The Arapaho were another group that was allied to the Sioux, and their ancestry may have at one time united them with the Cheyenne, although that is not known. They'd entered the state prior to European contact, but they, too, were relatively recent arrivals. They were a very small band, and war and starvation ultimately caused them to seek to enter the Wind River Reservation, which they were allowed to do. Today, they share the reservation with the Shoshone tribe.

The Blackfeet, who were present in northern Wyoming, were closely related to the Arapaho and, in fact, may have really been the same people. The fact that there's some question perhaps shows how little remains known about the history of certain groups. Their reputation in northwestern Wyoming was a fierce one, and they contested the Shoshone for control of that region.

Paiutes and Utes also entered Wyoming, although more on its fringes. These people, who seem to be rather ignored in the history of the Plains, also spoke an Utzo-Aztec language and therefore are related to the Shoshone in some fashion. Of course, not too much emphasis can be placed on mere language groups, as English and German are both Germanic languages in the Indo European language group, which has not meant for historic alliances.

The Comanche had their origin in Wyoming, as will be seen in the history of the Shoshone, a fact largely obscured by their later history. Their name dates back to their being the party that debated with the rest of the tribe about the adoption of the horse. They backed the immediate adoption, which their lifestyle thereafter attested to. The Shoshone would soon follow suit but not before a division in the people had somewhat occurred.

The Cherokee crossed Wyoming and left their name in the form of a trail.

A group largely and unfairly ignored in Wyoming's history is the Metis. We associate the Metis, a "mixed" group of people, mostly with western Canada today, but their range stretched far to the south and into the Powder River Basin, where they brought their Red River carts in order to hunt buffalo. Some claim that a few Metis may have been at Little Big Horn in 1876.

The native history of Wyoming is a rich but ongoing one, which is far too easy to forget. The Wind River Reservation has contracted since it was first formed, but it remains a very large landmass that is home to two groups of native peoples. Those people form a minority, but a sizable one, in Wyoming's population that continues to contribute to its history and character.

July 1

1861 The first stagecoaches to use the Northern (Central) Route via Forts Kearny, Laramie and Bridger begin to use that route, which was no doubt rather dangerous at the time.

1862 The United States outlaws polygamy by way of the Morrill Anti-Bigamy Act, which also grants large tracts of public land to the states with the directive to sell for the support of institutions teaching the mechanical and agricultural arts. It also obligated state male university students to military training. The education initiative resulted in sixty-eight land-grant colleges. This act led directly to the University of Wyoming (the land grant part, obviously).

The polygamy part of this was fairly obviously aimed at Mormon communities, principally in Utah but also in neighboring states.

1898 The pivotal battle of the Spanish-American War, the Battle of El Canay and San Juan Heights, sees the First U.S. Volunteer Cavalry—led at that time by its former second in command, Theodore Roosevelt— Seventeenth U.S. Infantry, Tenth U.S. Infantry, Twenty-first U.S. Infantry, Thirteenth U.S. Infantry and the Tenth U.S. Cavalry prevail. While Wyoming's Second Volunteer Cavalry remained in the United States, this epic event does have some association with Wyoming, as

First U.S. Volunteer Cavalry on Kettle Hill. *Library of Congress.*

some of the participants did. It also saw the completion of Theodore Roosevelt's rise to hero status, something that was particularly the case in the West. Also, there were a number of Wyoming citizens in the First U.S. Volunteer Cavalry, one Wyoming native in the Tenth U.S. Cavalry and another in the Seventeenth U.S. Infantry whose performance in action that day were quite notable. The Tenth U.S. Cavalry, it should be noted, was a segregated (i.e., black) unit whose officers were white.

Medal of Honor Citations from this event associated with Wyoming:

BAKER, EDWARD L., JR.: Sergeant major, Tenth U.S. Cavalry. Place and date: Santiago, Cuba, July 1, 1898. Birth: Laramie County, Wyoming. Date of issue: July 3, 1902. Citation: "Left cover and, under fire, rescued a wounded comrade from drowning."

Baker is a very unusual example of a black soldier in the segregated army, as he was promoted to the rank of captain following the Spanish-American War and retired at that rank in 1902. He was in a command position at that rank in the Forty-ninth Infantry.

ROBERTS, CHARLES D.: Second lieutenant, U.S. Army, Seventeenth U.S. Infantry. Place and date: El Caney, Cuba, July 1, 1898. Entered service at: Fort D.A. Russell, Wyoming. Birth: Fort D.A. Russell, Wyoming. Date of issue: June 21, 1899. Citation: "Gallantly assisted in the rescue of the wounded from in front of the lines under heavy fire of the enemy."

1919 The Volstead Act goes into effect. I can't help but note that Prohibition went into effect immediately prior to the big Fourth of July holiday. Wyoming had pushed the Volstead Act over the top with the vote of Senator F.E. Warren.

1920 A parachutist dies due to a parachute failure above the Casper airport.

1963 The Ninetieth Missile Wing is activated at Warren Air Force Base.

July 2

1862 President Lincoln signs an act granting land for state agricultural colleges. In its own way, this act would be as significant as the Homestead Acts in its impact on American society. Many state colleges and universities today owe their existence to this act, although the practical origins of these schools are often forgotten today.

1863 Chief Washakie signs the Fort Bridger Treaty of 1863.

July 3

1865 General Connor arrives at Fort Laramie with orders to protect the Overland Stage from Indian raids.

1868 The Wind River Reservation is created. Originally, the reservation was for the Shoshone tribe, whose leader, Washakie, had requested that the government set aside a reservation for his people. The Arapaho would come to call the reservation home some years thereafter.

1869 Sioux raid Wind River Valley but are driven off by soldiers.

1943 The Pole Mountain military reservation, formerly used for the training of Wyoming National Guard cavalrymen and cavalrymen from various posts around the region, is opened to civilian picnickers. That this would occur in 1943 says something about the direction the army was headed in at the time.

July 4 – Independence Day

1803 The Louisiana Purchase is announced to the American people.

1830 William Sublette names Rock Independence, as his Wind River–bound party spends the Fourth of July there. The name would shortly be changed to Independence Rock.

1836 Narcissa Prentiss Whitman and Eliza Hart Spaulding, the first European American women to cross the continent, make a marker at South Pass.

1866 Fort Halleck is abandoned.

1867 Cheyenne is named. On the same day, it was platted (and hence named) by General Grenville Dodge.

1874 The Second Cavalry engages Sioux/Cheyenne at Bad Water.

1908 The monument at the Fetterman battleground is dedicated.

1911 The aviation age arrives at Wyoming, with the first recorded flight in the state taking place in Gillette.

Fetterman Battleground
Monument. *Photograph
by the author.*

Fetterman Monument.
Photograph by the author.

July 5

1840 Father Pierre De Smet celebrates the first Catholic Mass observed in Wyoming.

1913 Big Piney is incorporated.

1937 Fort Laramie is officially declared to be public property to be turned over by the state to the federal government.

1937 A Rock Springs youth believes he heard a radio distress call from lost aviatrix Amelia Earhart, as reported in the Casper paper.

July 6

1863 John Bozeman leaves Fort Laramie to scout a trail to the Yellowstone Valley. The trail would become the Bozeman Trail.

1899 The Wyoming Battalion receives its orders in the Philippines to return to the United States.

July 7

1832 William Sublette's party reaches Jackson Hole and crosses Teton Pass.

1847 The first company of Mormon immigrants reaches Fort Bridger.

1864 Townsend wagon train is attacked near Platte Bridge Station.

1876 Sioux and Cheyenne attack an army scouting party at Sibley Lake in the Big Horn Mountains.

1907 The cornerstone of St. Mary's Cathedral in Cheyenne is laid.

St. Mary's Cathedral in Cheyenne. Cheyenne is the home of some of the oldest churches in Wyoming, which is not surprising given that it's one of the oldest towns in Wyoming. Many of the churches in downtown Cheyenne feature stone construction, with some of those churches dating to the late nineteenth or early twentieth century. *Photograph by the author.*

July 8

1889 Delegates are elected to the Wyoming Constitutional Convention.

1906 The last stage run over the Rawlins, Wyoming–Lander line is made.

July 9

1866 Colonel Henry B. Carrington leaves Fort Reno for Piney Creek to select the site for what became Fort Phil Kearny.

1915 The last stage robbery in the United States occurs in Yellowstone National Park, with financier Bernard among the passengers robbed.

July 10 — Wyoming Statehood Day

1866 The War Department issues orders to establish a fort south of Laramie. It was initially named Fort John Buford but was renamed Fort Sanders on September 5, 1866.

1890 Wyoming is admitted to the Union.

1933 Colonel Roche S. Mentzer, commanding officer of the 115th Cavalry, becomes ill at Fox Park in the Snowy Range and dies. That year, annual training had consisted of a protracted mounted march that took the mustered unit from Cheyenne to northern Colorado and then back into the Snowy Range.

Colonel Mentzer, in civilian life, was a lawyer in Cheyenne.

July 11

1862 The postmaster general of the United States orders mail carriers to forgo the trail over South Pass in favor of the Overland Trail due to the risk of Indian attacks.

July 12

1890 Lander is incorporated.

1900 The first Elks Lodge in Wyoming is chartered in Sheridan. Up until after World War II, fraternal lodges were a major feature of male life in most localities in the United States, with a very high percentage of American men belonging to some sort of fraternal organization.

1900 Basin sees a record high temperature for the state of 114 degrees Fahrenheit. It is no longer the record high, as 115 degrees was reached in Basin in 1983.

July 13

1866 Construction of Fort Phil Kearny begins.

Fort Kearny. The fort was destroyed by Indians following Red Cloud's War when the army abandoned it after the treaty ending the war. Its location has been excavated by the State of Wyoming, and it is now a Wyoming State Park. No original structures remain, but the outline of the fort and some of the foundations of the buildings can be seen. *Photograph by the author.*

July 14

1860 Owen Wister, the author of *The Virginian*, is born in Philadelphia. It is sometimes claimed that *The Virginian* was the first western novel, which it is not, but it was probably the first serious one. Wister's novel is completely set in Wyoming and is loosely based on the events that gave rise to the Johnson County War, although it takes the large cattleman's side, which most works of fiction have not. The

Owen Wister. Wister was a lawyer by training but not by inclination. His novel *The Virginian* was set entirely in Wyoming and has been translated into numerous languages around the globe. It remains in print and is one of the most copied novels of its genre, which it helped to create. *Library of Congress.*

novel itself has been used as the inspiration for numerous other works, including quite a few movies, but usually works based on it also reverse the protagonists. Wister's novel followed a visit to Wyoming, and the locations mentioned in it describe places he'd actually visited.

Wister would become a lawyer by education, but his practice period was brief, as he had no real affinity for the occupation. He is principally remembered today for his novel, but he wrote on other topics as well, including philosophy and politics. A close friend of Theodore Roosevelt, he can be identified politically with the Progressive movement.

July 15

1872 The cornerstone is laid for the territorial prison in Laramie.

1894 Butch Cassidy and Al Hainer are sent to the Wyoming State Penitentiary for extortion. They'd been running a protection racket aimed at ranchers.

July 16

1866 A discussion occurs between Colonel Carrington and Cheyenne at Fort Phil Kearny, resulting in a Cheyenne pledge of peace.

July 17

1866 Sioux warriors drive off a herd of livestock (175 horses and mules of the Eighteenth Infantry Regiment) at Fort Phil Kearney, with soldiers giving pursuit, resulting in some soldiers being killed and others wounded.

1921 Burnu Acquanetta is born near Cheyenne. She was an Arapaho and a minor movie actress.

July 18

1877 Cantonment Reno, then Fort McKinney on the Powder River, is moved to the north bank of Clear Creek.

1901 Tom Horn murders Willie Nickell, for which he is later hanged. In part, Horn is relatively rapidly identified due to leaving at the site an expended .30-30 cartridge, which was a rifle cartridge he was associated with. At the time, the .30-30 was regarded as a long-range, high-velocity cartridge, and it was a relatively new one as well. The murder was almost certainly a mistake, as Horn was very likely waiting for Willie's father. Willie was a big kid, albeit only fourteen, and was wearing his father's coat on the day of the murder.

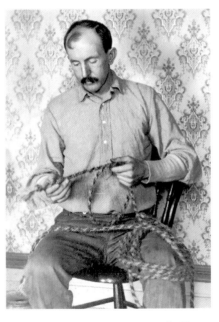

Tom Horn. This photo was taken while Horn was in prison. He was hanged with the rope he braided. *Courtesy of Wyoming State Archives, Department of State Parks and Cultural Resources.*

It's interesting to note that Horn was born in Missouri and grew up on a large family farm, although he left home as an early teen. His 1860 birth date would have caused him to grow up in the Missouri of the 1860s and 1870s, which was particularly lawless and produced a variety of notorious gunmen. He served as a civilian scout in the army under the legendary Al Sieber and saw service on both sides of the border. He picked up knowledge of the Apache language during this period.

In the period leading up to this infamous act, he seems to have been employed as an enforcer for certain cattle interests that were continuing to contest along the lines of the Johnson County War, as well as the ongoing sheep war. He first took up hiring out as a gunman in the Southwest after his service to the army. His role in Wyoming was often as a "stock detective," which gave a degree of legality to some of his activities.

His arrest and conviction is one of two instances in the first decade of the twentieth century in Wyoming in which the gunman was rapidly identified due to a cartridge preference, the other being the 1909 Spring Creek Raid, which was the last raid of Wyoming's long-running sheep wars. In that event, one of the assailants was armed with a semi-automatic Remington 1908 in .25 Remington, and his rifle was the only one of that type in the region.

Horn has remained an oddly popular and well-known figure in Wyoming's history and has his apologists. The reasons for this are not entirely clear. There are those who claim even to the present day that he was not guilty of the murder and was framed by those who had formerly employed him, citing the efforts of Joe Lefors, who was critical in tracking him down and supplying testimony against him. But the apologists' arguments do not stand up to scrutiny.

Looked at objectively, Horn was a late frontier-era figure who became ensnared in the violence of the period at the same time at which it was winding down. The same decade of his arrest would see Butch Cassidy and the Sundance Kid conclude their criminal activities in the state (also with Lefors playing a part in that) and the end of the sheep wars due to the arrival of effective law enforcement and unbiased juries. Perhaps Horn's role as a fin-de-siècle gunman plays a role in the ongoing fascination with him.

July 19

1867 The army commences construction of Fort Fetterman. The fort is located on a windy bluff overlooking the Platte River. The site requires those detailed to walk some distance to water, and for a period of time, the post would have the highest insanity rate in the army.

1885 Owen Wister takes his legendary snooze on the counter of the general store at Medicine Bow while waiting for a train. The Philadelphia-born Wister was very well educated and had hoped for a career in music but instead obtained a law degree from Harvard at the urging of his father. He practiced law in Philadelphia. During that period, he commenced vacationing in the West, with his first trip to Wyoming being this one in 1885. It would lead to his legendary book *The Virginian*.

1907 Isabel Jewell is born in Shoshoni. Jewell was a successful Broadway and screen actress in the 1930s and 1940s.

July 20

1862 Fort Halleck, near Elk Mountain, is established. It patrolled a section of the overland trails.

1866 A wagon train is attacked on Crazy Woman Creek by the Sioux and Cheyenne.

1889 Ellen "Cattle Kate" Watson and Jim Averell are hanged by area ranchers in the region of the Sweetwater River. This event has been one of the most enduring and controversial in Wyoming's history, with many different variants of it having been written. There are now so many variants that sorting out the truth is nearly impossible. It can't even be fully determined if Watson and Averell were married, which they might have been (they did take out a marriage license), or if Watson was a prostitute who took payment in cattle, which she might have been.

The murder is often placed in the context of the Johnson County War, where it doesn't properly belong.

It should be noted that this event is probably subject to more interpretation, evolution and revision than any other single event in Wyoming's history, much of it quite recent. For much of the twentieth century, Ellen Watson and Jim Averell were regarded as victims of an unwarranted extrajudicial lynching but not as totally innocent characters. The generally accepted view for many decades (and I believe the one that is recounted in the excellent *War on Powder River*) is that Watson was a prostitute (which does not preclude her being married to Averell) and that she took payment in cattle if no other currency was available. This got her into trouble with area ranchers, as the cattle were often stolen by the cowhands who paid for her services. Averell, according to this view, lost his life essentially for living with her and benefiting from her activities.

More recently, however, there have been serious, and not always entirely grounded, efforts to revive her reputation, and there have even been those who have viewed her as an early feminist businesswoman with a wholly legitimate business activity who was murdered simply for being a self-assertive woman. Frankly, that doesn't wash, and independent frontier women were not really novel. A more serious revisionist view holds that Averell and Watson were small-time homesteaders who were trespassing on the lands that were controlled by rancher Albert Bothwell. It may be that there is some truth to this view, which might also explain why the marriage of Averell and Watson was either not completed (a serious crime at that time) or kept secret, as it would have allowed both Averell and Watson to file separate homesteads.

Of course, it might be that both the earlier accepted version of events and the standard revisionist views are correct. Watson and Averell were homestead entrants, and that may have seriously irritated Bothwell and his companions, and Watson might also have been a prostitute.

Ella Watson.
*Courtesy of
Wyoming
State Archives,
Department
of State Parks
and Cultural
Resources.*

The vast expanse of time that has gone by since this 1889 event effectively means that the truth will never be really known now. What is undoubted is that Watson was the only woman ever lynched in Wyoming, and none of the perpetrators of the act made any effort to keep the deed secret. One even rode into Casper shortly after the news broke on the story, admitted his role and was basically left alone.

July 21

1867 Fort D.A. Russell is established outside Cheyenne on Crow Creek. It survives as an active duty military post today as Warren Air Force Base.

1885 Owen Wister is in Medicine Bow again, this time spending the night in the corner of a store.

1987 The most powerful tornado in Wyoming's history, the Teton-Yellowstone tornado, an F4, touches down in Yellowstone National Park and leaves a path of destruction one to two miles wide and twenty-four miles long while leveling fifteen thousand acres of mature pine forest.

July 22

1897 The Hole in the Wall fight between rustlers and ranchers happens near the Hole in the Wall.

1967 Wyomingite captain William B. Graves is shot down while piloting an OV-1C in Vietnam.

July 23

1874 George Custer climbs Inyan Kara Mountain in the Black Hills of Wyoming and carves his name there.

1888 Construction commences on the state penitentiary in Rawlins.

July 24

1832 Benjamin Bonneville leads the first wagon train to cross the Rocky Mountains at South Pass. Bonneville was an army officer on a two-year leave of absence, during which time he acted as a fur trader but also spent a great deal of time exploring.

1865 Sioux go into camp near Platte Bridge Station.

1866 The Battle of Clear Creek occurs near present-day Buffalo, where Indians besiege a wagon train. The wagon train was able to send word to Fort Phil Kearny and was relieved by a party of soldiers the following day.

July 25

1865 Lieutenant Bretney of Company G, Eleventh Ohio Cavalry, leaves Sweetwater Station with Captain A. Smyth Lybe of the Third U.S. Volunteer Infantry to go to Fort Laramie, about 150 miles away, to collect their unit's pay. On the way, they learned of the presence of Indian activity. They encountered Sergeant Amos Custard of the Eleventh Kansas Cavalry with a party of wagons about 25 miles west of Platte Bridge Station and encouraged him to proceed on that day with them, but Custard refused on the basis that his animals were tired. Bretney and Smyth would not arrive at Platte Bridge Station until 2:00 a.m.

1865 Sioux and Cheyenne attack Camp Dodge near present-day Casper.

1868 Congress passes an act creating the Wyoming Territory.

1895 Bannock Indians surround 250 settlers in Jackson Hole but are dispersed by the Ninth Cavalry. This was part of the Bannock War of 1895, which was spurred by the State of Wyoming prohibiting the killing of elk for their teeth and the subsequent arrest of several Bannock hunters that year.

July 26

1849 Company C, U.S. Mounted Rifles, arrives at Fort Laramie.

1865 On this day, two battles are fought in what is now Natrona County, Wyoming, with the first being fought in an attempt to avoid having the second occur.

The first battle is the Battle of Platte Bridge Station. Platte Bridge Station was one of a series of posts built on the Oregon Trail through Wyoming that guarded both the trail and the telegraph line that already ran alongside the trail by that time. It was garrisoned by men of the Eleventh Kansas Cavalry, as well as infantrymen from a galvanized Yankee unit.

Cheyenne, Sioux and Arapahos gathered outside the fort in the days immediately prior to it, just across from it in what is now Mills, Wyoming, in an attempt to draw the troops out. The Cheyenne and the Sioux were at war with the United States as a byproduct of the Sand Creek Massacre the prior winter. As a result of that, they had fled north into the Powder River Basin and had waged a war of raids. The strategy of trying to draw the soldiers out, which failed, is sometimes attributed to Crazy Horse, who may have been at the battle, although it is difficult to tell.

While the soldiers remained safely in the fort and the Indians abstained from assaulting it directly (as they usually did), it became necessary to try to move the tribesmen off, as an army wagon train was expected to arrive. When it was in sight, a relief party led by Lieutenant Caspar Collins, Eleventh Ohio Cavalry, crossed the bridge.

The battle was a short one, as the troopers were outnumbered and the combined Indian forces had the advantage of terrain. The Eleventh Kansas attempted to rapidly advance to the trail but was flanked by tribesmen from the hills who had been hidden in the area that is now Boatright Smith, a gravel contractor in Mills, Wyoming. Retreat was sounded, but several men were killed in the fight, including Collins. Stories about Collins's actions vary, but his horse is known to have turned into the advancing tribesmen. Some stated that he was attempting to rescue a wounded trooper. Others stated that his horse bolted. The Indian who acquired the horse later gave it away, as it was excessively rank.

Collins was not posted to Platte Bridge Station but had volunteered to lead the relief party after there had been some debate at the post about who should do it. That has remained an enduring controversy. He wore his full uniform, frock coat and all, on the hot July day, as he did not expect to survive the battle.

The second battle is the Battle of Red Buttes, which occurred within sight of Platte Bridge Station after the Battle of Platte Bridge Station. This battle occurred when the tribesmen discovered the wagon train that was coming east down the Oregon Trail on its way from the stations at Independence Rock and Sweetwater Station. Troopers of the Eleventh Kansas Cavalry who were posted with the horse herd some miles away in Bessemer Bend had attempted to dissuade the wagon train, with men of the Second Infantry, from going on, as they had seen the large Indian party. But Sergeant Custard, who was in command of the wagon train, insulted the cavalrymen, declaring them to be cowards, and proceeded on. Custard, a veteran of fighting in the East during the Civil War, shared the common trait that many with similar experience had and greatly underestimated the fighting capacity of native inhabitants. When the wagon train neared the post and the Indians noticed it, they attacked it and killed nearly every soldier, save for a few with the train. A very few managed to escape on horseback, cross the Platte and make their way to Platte Bridge Station.

A grand total of twenty-six U.S. troops were killed in the combined battles, with twenty-one of those being at Red Buttes. The mass grave of those who died at Red Buttes has been lost. The town of Mills has undoubtedly grown out toward that location, and now Casper is as well.

In recognition of his heroism, Platte Bridge Station was renamed Fort Caspar, with the term "fort" recognizing the more important and permanent nature of the post over that of a "station." Collins's first name was used rather than his last, as the name Collins had already attached to Fort Collins in Colorado, named after General Collins, Caspar's father. The honor was in some ways short-lived, as the post

Monument to Caspar Collins in Casper, Wyoming, which is named for Collins but spelled his name incorrectly. *Photograph by the author.*

was abandoned as part of the agreement that ended Red Cloud's War. It was revived, however, when the town of Casper was founded a couple decades later, albeit with a different spelling.

July 27

1901 The first smelter opens at Grand Encampment.

1920 William Jennings Bryan speaks in Casper.

1922 A grasshopper infestation darkens Sheridan's skies.

1922 The first recorded ascent of Mount Moran occurs.

2013 National Day of the Cowboy is celebrated. Wyoming is the first state to recognize the day.

July 28

1865 The Powder River Campaign commences. The campaign, under the command of Brigadier General Patrick E. Connor, was to "rein in the Arapaho, Cheyenne and Sioux."

1908 The Star, a Casper livery stable, burns down. The fire was kept from spreading but was a major disaster in the town, resulting in the loss of eleven horses, a hearse and a large amount of feed.

July 29

1872 The first claimed assent of the Grand Teton is completed. Nathaniel P. Langford and James Stevenson made the claim, but it is disputed, with some feeling that they reached a side peak.

July 30

1869 The first census of Wyoming Territory is completed.

July 31

1867 Fort Fetterman is given that name. It was only in its second week of existence.

1868 Fort Phil Kearny is abandoned. It wouldn't be around for long after that.

1892 Legendary Wyoming geologist and University of Wyoming geology professor Samuel H. Knight is born. His parents moved to Laramie in 1893, so he was associated with Laramie his entire life, save for attending Columbia for his doctorate and his service in World War I. The geology building at the University of Wyoming is named after him.

1898 Wyoming volunteers, the Wyoming Battalion, land at Manila and disembark from the *Ohio*.

1899 The Wyoming Battalion, having been in the Philippines for exactly one year, embarks on the Grant at Manila and starts its journey home.

1914 Twenty-five Yellowstone coaches are robbed.

Sidebar:
World War II and Wyoming

World War II was such a colossal war that its impact on the United States as a whole is almost incalculable. Wyoming was no exception. The war impacted the state in the same ways that it impacted the rest of the nation while at the same time having some unique regional impacts.

Nearly every able-bodied young man—and indeed quite a few able-bodied middle-aged men—served in the military during those years. By the war's end, men were entering right out of high school, with some leaving high school to enter the service. A good friend of mine's father, for example, entered the army prior to completing high school, a fairly common story in those days. And as noted, it wasn't just young men. The legal community, for example, in Wyoming was seriously depleted by so many lawyers entering the service. There's actually one Wyoming Supreme Court legal opinion of the period noting that one of the appellate parties' lawyers was absent due to being in the service and that the party was therefore appearing pro se (without lawyer), but that they were certain that had the lawyer been there, the party would have been well represented. It should be noted, by the way, that entering the service with a JD at that time did not mean a direct commission for the lawyer, and plenty of lawyers served in the war as enlisted men.

The first group of Wyoming soldiers to enter the service did so as National Guardsmen in 1940. Most of Wyoming's Guardsmen were in the 115th Cavalry (Horse Mechanized). The unit was a pioneering one, reflecting an army attempt to blend horse cavalry with mechanized cavalry, which received high marks by none other than Lucian Truscott, one of the stars of the Allied effort in North Africa and Italy. Mobilized in 1940, as noted, the unit was not actually sent overseas until late 1944, by which time only a few Wyomingites remained in the unit and by which time it was a mechanized cavalry unit. Most of the Wyoming troopers had been cadred out of the unit into others well before that, after having spent the first couple months after Pearl Harbor patrolling the Pacific Coast. The unit, which had been a popular one for membership on the part of high school students prior to the war, saw more than its share of former members who went on to distinguished service in other units of the army and army air corps. Two of the former members whom I had the honor of meeting had been pilots in the army air corps.

Officers of the 115th Cavalry (Horse Mechanized) in Fort Lewis, Washington. *Courtesy of the Wyoming Militia Historical Society.*

Probably for these reasons, World War II is one war that has a monument somewhere in nearly every Wyoming community commemorating servicemen who fought in the war. Many communities have memorials that list every single soldier, sailor, marine and coast guardsman who served from the county.

The war visited Wyoming in ways other than through the numerous servicemen the state contributed. The state had at least four active bases during the war, two of which predated the war. Fort F.E. Warren had been a long-standing army base outside Cheyenne, having originally been named Fort D.A. Russell. The post had shared a huge training range with the National Guard between Cheyenne and Laramie in the form of the Pole Mountain Training Area. It remained a training range into the war, although the National Guard had just established a separate training range at Guernsey. The guard had just been able to use that facility for a single season prior to the war starting. F.E. Warren was used for a variety of purposes during the war. Some soldiers received basic training there. A Quartermaster Replacement Training Center was headquartered there and operated at Pole Mountain.

The army also had a preexisting facility outside Sheridan in the form of Fort MacKenzie. Fort MacKenzie was a remount station, a facility that trained horses, and more particularly, it was the regional headquarters for purchasing them. Horses and mules remained significant to the army throughout the war, with mules becoming increasingly important just as the importance of horses decreased. Sheridan had long been a very "horsey" area, making it a natural for a remount station. This facility would close shortly after the war, its purpose having been rendered obsolete. Its grounds are now the property of the State Veteran's Administration hospital.

Casper saw a base created in the form of the Army Air Corps Casper Air Base. The base trained bomber crews. The substantial air base grounds are now those of the Natrona County International Airport. The facility was substantial enough to have a satellite base in Scottsbluff, Nebraska. Natrona County had another long-standing military facility, the Naval Petroleum Oil Reserve, which was a federal reservation formed to store oil for the navy's use. That facility still exists, although it no longer serves that function.

Converse County had a prisoner of war camp located at Douglas. The camp contained German and Italian prisoners of war. Only one building of that facility remains. I haven't seen it, but apparently it contains murals painted by Italian prisoners. A couple of the surviving buildings from the Casper Air Base likewise feature murals, albeit painted by airmen artists.

Another type of internment camp existed during the war at Heart Mountain, near Cody. Heart Mountain War Relocation Center was an internment camp for Japanese Americans who were kept in such camps if they had previously been living on the Pacific Coast. Today, it is a historic site dedicated to the memory of those who were kept there during the war.

Wyoming's industry also played a role in the war. Cheyenne had a facility that constructed nose turrets for the B-17 bomber. An important modification to that design occurred there, leading to the nickname for the turret design being the "Cheyenne Turret." Uranium was mined in a quarry just outside Laramie and partially processed just outside town at a facility that is still visible for use in the early stages of the Manhattan Project. The oil industry, of course, played a major role in the war, as the United States was an oil exporter at that time. Likewise, coal was an important war material produced within the state.

Agriculture employed a higher percentage of Wyomingites at that time than it does now and was a vital part of the war economy. Agricultural workers were exempt from the draft as critical war workers, although almost every young cowboy volunteered anyhow. The Holscher Meat Packing plant in Casper was engaged in military contracts, among others, during the war. Wool production was vital at a time when every soldier was issued at least some wool uniforms and the soldiers in Europe wore wool every day.

Finally, the war changed things in ways that we can hardly recognize now unless we lived through them, which most of us did not. The war had a massive impact on the mobility of society that World

War I had not, and to a large extent, the concept of Americans as mobile people who grow up in one place and then leave to work in another, or many others, came about during the war. Americans were relatively mobile, of course, prior to the war but not like they were after the war. The war, or rather the aftermath of the war, also sent many people to college and university through the GI Bill. Many sections of society found college available to them for the very first time. That trend only continued to develop after the war, with not attending college being unthinkable for many in our modern society. Before the war, entire demographic groups rarely went to college. The World War II generation was, for a large percentage of Americans, the first generation to attend university.

Technological developments during the war ended up revolutionizing how Wyomingites traveled, although for the most part they likely generally are not aware of that today. Before the war, most families in the state had a car, and some more than one, but those cars and trucks were all two-wheel-drive vehicles. The 4x4 vehicle really got its start because of the Second World War, as Jeep and Ford made thousands upon thousands of Jeeps and Dodge made thousands of trucks of a type that would become the postwar Power Wagon. The widespread road accessibility of the country from late fall through late spring came about because of World War II. Also because of that, however, the need for backcountry cowboys or even home ranch cowboys was greatly reduced, working a revolution in agriculture that destroyed the jobs of hundreds of cowboys. Indeed, Wyoming's ranches, already growing due to the stress placed on small ranches by the Great Depression, were able to continue that trend in part for that reason. One rancher and his family could now cover ground that it had taken several cowboys to do in winter before, and that was even true to a lesser degree in the summer.

In short, no war since the Indian Wars impacted Wyoming so much as World War II. Memorials to the war are located in every county, and no wonder. The impact of the war was vast and remains so.

And as a final note, Wyoming even was the site of a Japanese bombing of sorts. A Japanese high-altitude, unmanned balloon made it all the way to Wyoming. These were designed to start fires, and upon landing, it actually did, although the impact was nonexistent. The existence of this Japanese effort was kept secret throughout the war in an effort to keep the public from panicking about it.

AUGUST IN WYOMING

August is a hot month in Wyoming, at least by Wyoming's standards. Temperatures range up to the nineties. Water begins to become in short supply in dry years. But the end of the month usually starts to see cooler temperatures, with a promise of even cooler temperatures to come.

August 1

1915 Automobiles are first admitted into Yellowstone National Park.

1927 Guernsey Dam is completed.

1953 The movie *Shane* is released. The film, regarded as a western classic, was filmed in Jackson Hole. The movie is based very loosely on the events of the Johnson County War and has remained popular all these years. It's been subject to some wild interpretations as a result. Like most movies that use the basic story of the Johnson County War as inspiration, it presents a heroic vision of the small, helpless farmer (rather than small rancher) who is pitted against merciless large ranchers. Sets and costumes used in the film are mixed with regard to their authenticity, with the large cattlemen being most accurately depicted in regards to their appearance. Jack Palance's gunman is particularly accurately attired.

Probably demonstrating my contrarian streak, I always root for the large cattlemen in the film.

1957 The United States and Canada create the North American Aerospace Defense Command (NORAD). This is significant to Wyoming in that F.E. Warren AFB has long had strategic missile wings.

1959 Wyoming's artillery and armor National Guard units are consolidated into the Forty-ninth Field Artillery Battalion, which I was in back in the old days.

1985 The worst flood in Wyoming's history occurs in Cheyenne when the town is struck by a severe thunderstorm. Property loss was $65 million in 1985 dollars. Twelve deaths and seventy injuries occurred, with particularly horrific flooding in downtown Cheyenne. The event happened in the evening, and people were caught unawares, including attendees of a downtown Cheyenne movie theater.

August 2

1867 Just one day after a nearly identical event occurred outside Fort C.F. Smith, the northernmost fort on the Bozeman Trail, Ninth Infantry repulse a Sioux and Cheyenne attack in the mountains near Fort Phil Kearney in the Wagon Box Fight, a battle again demonstrating the superiority of the new breech-loading rifles over the muzzleloading rifle. The soldiers were grossly outnumbered during the fight.

1887 Rowell Hodge receives a patent for barbed wire, an invention that would make fencing the range practical and massively change western ranching and farming.

August 3

1867 Troops are dispatched from Fort Phil Kearny to establish Fort C.F. Smith.

August 4

1876 Frank E. Lucas, the thirteenth governor of Wyoming upon the death of Governor William B. Ross in 1924, is born in Grant City, Missouri. Upon his defeat by Nellie Tayloe Ross, he returned to his adopted town of Buffalo and became the editor of the *Buffalo Bulletin*. His term as governor was a mere matter of months in length.

August 5

1917 The entire National Guard, only recently released from duty due to the crisis with Mexico and then recalled due to the outbreak of World War I, is conscripted into the U.S. Army. The technicality of conscription was necessary due to an attorney general's opinion that the National Guard could not serve overseas.

August 6

1898 The Wyoming Battalion leaves the steamer *Ohio* in Manila Bay and goes into camp at Paranaque.

1910 Crystal Lake Dam is completed.

August 7

1886 Fort Fred Steele is deactivated. A town remained behind where the fort had been and survived for many decades until the Lincoln Highway bypassed it.

1892 The Johnson County invaders plead not guilty in Cheyenne to the charges against them.

1914 Jackson is incorporated.

August 8

1929 Major Doyen P. Wardwell of Casper, a World War I veteran of the Lafayette Escadrille and a pioneer Wyoming aviator, dies in an airplane crash. The Wardwell Addition to the City of Casper would be named after him, and the Casper Municipal Airport was renamed for him. That airport later formed some of the city streets for Bar Nunn, Wyoming.

1936 Ernest Hemingway visits Laramie. He visited Wyoming and the Rocky Mountains fairly frequently.

August 9

1832 The stockade at Fort Bonneville is completed.

August 10

1886 Cavalry arrive at Yellowstone to police the park.

1912 Congress appropriates $45,000 for the purchase of lands and maintenance of a winter elk refuge in Jackson Hole, where ranchers, and then the state, had been undertaking feeding the elk during winter. The National Elk Refuge continues to this day. Not only are elk fed during the hard winter months, but also the feeding of the elk can be toured by way of horse-drawn sleds.

August 11

1865 General Patrick Connor establishes Camp Conner in the Powder River Basin. It would later become Fort Reno.

1898 William O. Owen (federal surveyor and outdoorsman), Franklin Spalding, Frank Petersen and John Shive reach the summit of Mount Owen of the Grand Tetons, the first documented climb of that peak. The climb was sponsored by a climbing association, the Rocky Mountain Club. Publication of the news in the *New York Herald* met with an immediate spat between Owen and Nathaniel P. Landford. Landford, together with James Stevenson, claimed to have reached the summit on July 29, 1872. However, their description and sketches seem to match the summit of the Enclosure (named after a man-made rock palisade of unknown Indian construction), a side peak of Grand Teton. The debate continues on, as it is not possible to discount or prove Landford's earlier claim, while Owen's later one is an established fact.

Somewhat missed in this debate is that another rival claim exists on the part of Captain Charles Kieffer, Private Logan Newell and Private John Rhyan, who may have climbed the peak on September 10, 1893, using the difficult Exum Ridge Route. These soldiers were all stationed at Fort Yellowstone and, according to a letter sent from Kieffer to Owen after Owen's assent, were accompanied by his depiction. Kieffer indicated that the three soldiers attempted the climb a second time later but failed due to early snows. It's interesting to note that Owen did not publish or reveal the letter, and it came to light only when it was uncovered in the Owen papers at the Western History Research Center, University of Wyoming–Laramie, by Leigh N. Ortenburger in the spring of 1959.

The dispute will never be settled, but I suspect that the army party was the first one.

1946 The Wyoming Air National Guard is organized.

August 12

1877 Public land offices in Evanston are opened.

1942 Internees begin to arrive at the Heart Mountain Relocation Center.

1945 The wreckage of a B-17 that crashed into bomber mountain on June 28, 1943, is discovered, along with the remains of the crew, by two cowboys.

August 13

1806 John Colter is honorably discharged from the U.S. Army two months early in order to allow him to depart the Corps of Discovery and lead two trappers back up the Upper Missouri.

1898 Colorado and Wyoming volunteer infantry raise the U.S. flag for the first time over Manila.

1927 Tim McCoy begins filming the movie *Wyoming*. He moved to Wyoming after college and was briefly the adjutant general of the Wyoming National Guard.

August 14

1848 Congress creates the Oregon Territory, which included parts of Wyoming. Unlike the later state maps, the eastern and western edges of the territory were based on topographic features.

1897 Road agents dressed as cavalrymen stop fifteen stagecoaches in Yellowstone National Park, robbing items from most of them. The victims included an army paymaster and his escort, who mistook the agents for soldiers.

1923 An explosion at the Frontier Mine in Kemmerer kills ninety-nine people.

August 15

1842 John C. Fremont raises the Stars and Stripes from the top of the Wind River Range, naming the location Fremont's Peak.

August 16

1825 Wyoming's first delegate to Congress, Stephen F. Nuckolls, is born in Grayson County, Virginia.

August 17

1869 Major John Wesley Powell's party passes Sentinel Peak overlooking the Grand Canyon. It had left Green River on May 24.

August 18

1872 The Hayden Expedition camps at Geyser Basin in Yellowstone.

1916 Fire destroys coal chutes and four freight cars that belonged to the Chicago & Northwestern Railroad Company in Douglas.

August 19

1854 Lieutenant John L. Grattan, Sixth U.S. Infantry, and thirty of his men are killed by Sioux Indians at a location on the Oregon Trail not far from Fort Laramie. The fight is regarded as sort of an early western Plains Indian fight and an indication of things to come. The entire episode was over a cow belonging to a Mormon Oregon Trail migrant that had been taken by one of the Sioux and killed. The Sioux had offered reparations in the form of the migrant's choice of a horse out of the Indian herd, which had been refused. Grattan, who led a detachment to the Sioux camp the following day, handled the matter very poorly, and things got out of hand, whereupon shots were fired by the soldiers and returned by the much more numerous Sioux.

Grattan's entire command of thirty soldiers was killed in the battle to the loss of one Sioux, Conquering Bear, who was the Sioux chief of the band in question and who was likely killed with the very first shot of the battle. The Sioux made a token pass at Fort Laramie the following day and then dispersed. The army recalled William S. Harney from Paris in order to send him to the field with the Second Dragoons as a result, but they did not take the field until the following August, an entire year later, giving an idea of the slowness of events in the nineteenth century.

One of the less noted but very notable aspects of this story: Rather than retaliating, the U.S. Army declared that

Grattan had exceeded his authority. An explosive situation was not allowed to escalate, but the seeds of distrust and future violence had been sown. Grattan had handled the entire situation very badly. But the army, in its follow-up, was wise to regard his actions as improper, in spite of the disaster it was to his men.

1878 Robert Widdowfield and Union Pacific detective Tip Vincent are killed in the line of duty by Big Nose George Parrott's gang near Elk Mountain. Widdowfield and Vincent were attempting to apprehend the gang that had tried to rob a train.

1950 The 300th AFA, Wyoming Army National Guard, is federalized for service in the Korean War.

August 20

1988 This day is known as "Black Saturday" of the Yellowstone fire, in which more than 150,000 acres were burned in a firestorm.

August 21

1937 Fifteen firefighters are killed and thirty-eight injured in the Blackwater forest fire near Cody. Those who lost their lives were:

Alfred G. Clayton, ranger South Fork District, Shoshone NF, age forty-five

James T. Saban, CCC technical foreman, Tensleep Camp F-35, age thirty-six

Rex A. Hale Jr., assistant to the technician, Shoshone NF, from the Wapiti CCC camp, age twenty-one

Paul E. Tyrrell Jr., forester, Bighorn NF (Foreman), age twenty-four

Billy Lea, Bureau of Public Roads crewman

John B. Gerdes, CCC Enrollee, Tensleep Camp F-35

Will C. Griffith, CCC Enrollee, Tensleep Camp F-35

Mack T. Mayabb, CCC Enrollee, Tensleep Camp F-35

George E. Rodgers, CCC Enrollee, Tensleep Camp F-35

Roy Bevens, CCC Enrollee, Tensleep Camp F-35

Clyde Allen, CCC Enrollee, Tensleep Camp F-35

Ernest Seelke, CCC Enrollee, Tensleep Camp F-35

Rubin Sherry, CCC Enrollee, Tensleep Camp F-35

William Whitlock, CCC Enrollee, Tensleep Camp F-35

Ambrogio Garza, CCC Enrollee, Tensleep Camp F-35

August 22

1877 Nez Perce enter Yellowstone National Park during their flight toward Canada.

1912 Casper's first purpose-built movie theater opens.

August 23

1842 John C. Fremont carves his name on Independence Rock.

1868 Episcopal Bishop Randall consecrates St. Mark's Parish in Cheyenne, the first known consecration of a church in Wyoming.

1949 The Wyoming Stock Growers Association donates a collection of its historic materials to the University of Wyoming.

1965 The state dedicates restored buildings at Fort Fetterman. This does not mean that the entire post was restored. Only two restored buildings are present. They are used to house displays. The foundations of other buildings are clearly visible but are all down to ground level.

August 24

1842 John C. Fremont's raft capsizes in the rapids in what is now Fremont Canyon, dumping most of his party's scientific instruments.

1865 Companies C and D of the Fifth U.S. Volunteers (Galvanized Yankees) relieve the Sixth Michigan Cavalry at Fort Reno.

August 25

1850 Western humorist Edgar Wilson "Bill" Nye is born in Maine. His career as a humorist was launched while he was a postmaster in Laramie.

1972 Congress authorizes the John D. Rockefeller Jr. Memorial Parkway.

2010 Governor Dave Freudenthal signs an executive order increasing the protected sage grouse habitat by a net of 400,000 acres.

August 26

1917 A new producing oil well comes in at the Salt Creek Field. The field was highly active during World War I, and a regional oil boom also occurred, along with a horse boom, because of the war. There was as a result a great deal of construction in downtown Casper during this era.

August 27

1883 President Arthur begins a tour of Yellowstone National Park.

Above: Chester A. Arthur and party in Yellowstone. *Library of Congress*.

Opposite: General Stager, part of the president's party, doing some fishing in Yellowstone. Apparently, limits were not a concern. *Library of Congress*.

1910 Theodore Roosevelt is present in Cheyenne for Frontier Days.

August 28

1865 Fort Connor is established by General Patrick Connor, Sixth Michigan Cavalry. The Sixth Michigan Cavalry was serving in Wyoming at the time. The fort was renamed Fort Reno for late major general Jesse L. Reno later that year. The fort was abandoned in 1868 as a condition of the peace treaty that resulted in the end of Red Cloud's War, which is generally regarded as the only Plains Indian war that resulted in a clear-cut Indian victory.

1868 Fort Reno is abandoned.

August 29

1865 General Connor leads 125 Michigan cavalrymen and 90 Pawnee in an early morning assault on an Arapaho village encamped on the Tongue River in the last battle of the Powder River Expedition. The battle was at the current location of the town of Ranchester. At the time of the assault, many of the Arapaho men were away fighting the Crow Indians along the Big Horn River, although the cavalrymen and their Pawnee scouts were nonetheless outnumbered.

The fighting lasted all day, and Connor had to bring up two howitzers to repel an Arapaho counterattack designed to hold Connor's force back while the Arapaho withdrew their camp, which included the remaining older men, women and children. Sixty-three Arapaho were killed in the battle, and eighteen women and children were taken prisoner but subsequently released. One thousand Arapaho horses were taken and killed.

The battle is notable for several peculiar reasons. For one thing, while Connor's forces were in the field to address Indian raiding that had gone on earlier that year, it appears that the Arapaho, who were a very small band of Indians, were not at war with the United States, or at least this band was not. So the assault, while conceived of by Connor as an attack on a hostile band, was in fact an assault on a peaceful band. The assault would turn them hostile, however, and they would be allied with the Sioux and Cheyenne up through the 1870s.

1870 Mount Washburn in Yellowstone National Park is ascended for the first time by members of the Washburn-Langford-Doane Expedition. The scientific/topographic expedition was under a military escort led by U.S. Army Cavalry officer lieutenant Gustavus Cheyney Doane, who made this report:

The view from the summit is beyond all adequate description. Looking northward from the base of the mountain the great plateau stretches away to the front and left with its innumerable groves and sparkling waters, a variegated landscape of surpassing beauty, bounded on its extreme verge by the cañons of the Yellowstone. The pure atmosphere of this lofty region causes every outline of tree, rock or lakelet to be visible with wonderful distinctness, and objects twenty miles away appear as if very near at hand. Still further to the left the snowy ranges on the headwaters of Gardiner's river stretch away to the westward, joining those on the head of the Gallatin, and forming, with the Elephant's Back, a continuous chain, bending constantly to the south, the rim of the Yellowstone Basin. On the verge of the horizon appear, like mole hills in the distance, and far below, the white summits above the Gallatin Valley. These never thaw during the summer months, though several thousand feet lower than where we now stand upon the bare granite and no snow visible near, save in the depths of shaded ravines. Beyond the plateau to the right front is the deep valley of the East Fork bearing away eastward, and still beyond, ragged volcanic peaks, heaped in inextricable confusion, as far as the limit of vision extends. On the east, close beneath our feet, yawns the immense gulf of the Grand Cañon, cutting away the bases of two mountains in forcing a passage through the range. Its yellow walls divide the landscape nearly in a straight line to the junction of Warm Spring Creek below. The ragged edges of the chasm are from two hundred to five hundred yards apart, its depth so profound that the river bed is no where visible. No sound reaches the ear from the bottom of the abyss; the sun's rays are reflected on the further wall and then lost in the darkness below. The mind struggles and then falls back upon itself despairing in the effort to grasp by a single thought the idea of its immensity. Beyond, a gentle declivity, sloping from the summit of the broken range, extends to the limit of vision, a wilderness of unbroken pine forest.

1900 The Hole in the Wall Gang robs a train near Tipton.

August 30

1877 Cantonment Reno is renamed Fort McKinney.

The location of Cantonment Reno today. *Photograph by the author.*

1890 The first oil strike at the Salt Creek field.

August 31

1865 A road-building party under the command of Colonel J.A. Sawyer, which includes eighty-two wagons, is attacked by Arapahos in reaction to having been attacked on the Tongue River by General Connor the day prior. The regrouped Arapahos conducted a thirteen-day siege on the party, which moved somewhat during the first two days but was immobilized by September 2.

SEPTEMBER IN WYOMING

September is a month in Wyoming that alternates between warm and cool. In many years, the first significant snowstorms come in September. The early hunting seasons begin, and sportsmen begin to think of taking the field for the fall. It's also the month when stockmen begin to think of bringing their stock down from the high country.

September 1

1903 Cheyenne's first automobile is delivered.

1927 Charles Lindbergh lands the Spirit of St. Louis in Cheyenne.

September 2

1885 In one of the worst examples of race-based violence in western U.S. history, 150 white miners in Rock Springs brutally attack their Chinese co-workers, killing 28, wounding 15 others and driving several hundred more out of town. Governor Warren intervened to stop further bloodshed by having federal troops sent to Rock Springs, and he himself went there and to Evanston, where it appeared that the violence might spread.

September 3

1865 Colonel Nelson Cole, with troops from Missouri, engages Sioux, Arapaho and Cheyenne on Dry Fork in the Powder River Basin.

1885 Governor Warren arrives in Rock Springs by train following the previous day's violent riots.

1918 The first uranium discovery in Wyoming is announced, with the discovery having been made near Lusk.

September 4

1945 Two new Civil Air Patrol Squadrons are formed, one in Kemmerer and one in Evanston. The Civil Air Patrol is the official auxiliary of the U.S. Air Force. It had its origin in World War II, when the decision was made to employ the nation's light civil aircraft fleet for anti-submarine patrols. The organization was kept after World War II for the purpose of search and rescue and continues to exist today for that purpose. It has a cadet branch that exists as a species of Air Force Jr. ROTC but without the connection with specific schools like regular Jr. ROTC.

2007 The Wyoming state quarter is released.

2007 The first academic course class for freshmen occurs at Wyoming Catholic University.

September 5

1866 Fort John Buford is renamed Fort Sanders.

1879 The Delmonico Hotel and Washington Market collapse in Cheyenne, killing several people.

1885 U.S. Army troops arrive in Rock Springs following anti-Chinese rioting.

1894 The first Jewish wedding in Wyoming occurs in Cheyenne.

September 6

1870 Laramie's Eliza A. Swain becomes the first woman to legally cast a vote in the United States.

1887 The University of Wyoming opens. It had, at the time, forty-two students and five faculty members.

September 7

1870 Nathaniel P. Langford sketches the first detailed map of Yellowstone Lake from the vantage point of Colter Peak.

1873 Captain W.A. Jones names Togwotee Pass after his Sheepeater (Mountain Shoshone) guide, Togwotee.

September 8

1851 Negotiations that would lead to the Horse Creek Treaty of 1851 between Plains Indians and the United States begin on Horse Creek, thirty miles east of Fort Laramie.

1867 The army post located on Crow Creek near Cheyenne is named Fort D.A. Russell.

1943 The first female lookout is assigned in the Medicine Bow National Forest. Perhaps it is coincidence, but this event occurred during World War II, when women were occupying many traditional male occupations due to labor shortages.

1978 Yellowstone National Park is designated a United Nations World Heritage Site.

September 9

1885 Additional U.S. troops arrive in Wyoming due to the Rock Springs Massacre. They escort Chinese workers, against their desires, back to Rock Springs.

1886 Construction commences on the Wyoming State Capitol, although the cornerstone would not be laid until the following year.

1920 Cheyenne's airport sees its first airmail flight.

September 10

1889 Newcastle is founded by the Lincoln Land Company, a subsidiary of the Chicago, Burlington & Quincy.

September 11—Patriot Day

1890 The first election is held in Wyoming to elect state officeholders. Francis E. Warren is elected governor.

1988 The first snows in Yellowstone National Park begin to dampen the huge forest fire that has been going on there since July.

September 12

1857 U.S. Topographical Engineer lieutenant G.K. Warren causes a camp to be erected in the Black Hills. The camp included a stockade and was named Camp Jenney.

September 13

1942 Responding to calls from the commander of the Army Air Corps Casper Air Base, city officials take steps to close the Sandbar, Casper's infamous red-light district. Almost remembered in a nostalgic, semi-charming manner today, the Sandbar had been a concentration of vice for Natrona County since the 1920s where criminal activity was openly conducted. In spite of the World War II effort, the Sandbar remained a center for the conduct of vice until the 1970s, at which point it was attacked by an urban renewal project that effectively destroyed its infrastructure.

1953 Neil McNeice discovers uranium in the Gas Hills, which will lead ultimately to mining in that district.

September 14

1950 President Truman signs a bill merging most of Jackson Hole National Monument into Grand Teton National Park.

September 15

1885 Governor Warren requests that federal troops sent to Rock Springs following attacks on Chinese miners be withdrawn from that town.

1904 One thousand sheep are disemboweled by masked raiders in one of the raids of the sheep war. This occurred near Daniel.

September 16

1811 The Astorians rename Seeds-Kee-Dee-Agie (Prairie Hen River) the Spanish River. It would later be renamed the Green River.

1924 A coal mine explosion at Kemmerer kills fifty-five.

1950 War Memorial Stadium opens at the University of Wyoming.

September 17—
U.S. Constitution Day

1851 The Fort Laramie Treaty of 1851 is signed between United States treaty commissioners and representatives of the Cheyenne, Sioux, Arapaho, Crow, Shoshone, Assiniboine, Mandan, Hidatsa and Arikara nations. Of note, not all these tribes were typically at peace among themselves. The treaty set forth traditional territorial claims of the tribes among themselves, guaranteed safe passage for settlers on the Oregon Trail and provided for return on an annuity in the amount of $50,000 for fifty years. It also provided for the establishment of roads and forts on Indian territory.

The United States Senate ratified the treaty but adjusted compensation from fifty to ten years. Acceptance of the revisions was forthcoming from all the tribes except the Crow, who ironically were generally regarded as U.S. allies but more accurately were Sioux enemies.

This treaty should properly be regarded as a failure. Not all the promised payments were forthcoming. The payments, while not at all unsubstantial by nineteenth-century standards, were likely not well understood by the intended recipients. The general acceptance of the Indian tribes was questionable to a degree, as the ability of any one group of delegates to ratify anything for an entire tribe was questionable. The United States failed to accurately gauge the degree of western movement that would occur in the

1850s and 1860s, as it could not have predicted the impact of gold strikes in the West and then the mass migration caused by the Civil War, so it was completely ineffectual in restricting migration to the Oregon Trail.

1865 Sergeant Charles L. Thomas of Company E, Eleventh Ohio Cavalry, "carried a message through a country infested with hostile Indians and saved the life of a comrade en route, which won him the Medal of Honor. Thomas was with General Connor's Powder River Expedition, in Wyoming, at the time.

What's missed in the official account is that General Patrick Connor called for a volunteer "to go as a scout and find Cole or perish in the attempt." Thomas volunteered. Colonel Cole, who was hoping for relief, was surrounded with his command at the time, as a patrol had revealed. Sergeant Thomas was to deliver a message back to him, traveling 201 miles alone over a thirty-six-hour period. Part of the time Thomas was under fire, and he actually captured an Indian pony en route and took it along with his own. He ended up delivering the Indian pony to a soldier of the Second Missouri he encountered en route and took him along the remainder of the way to Cole's camp.

1945 The first classes are held at Casper College. The college occupied the top floor of Natrona County High School for the first years of its existence.

September 18

1870 Old Faithful is given that name by members of the Washburn-Langford-Doane Expedition.

September 19

1900 The Wild Bunch robs the First National Bank of Winnemucca, Nevada.

September 20

1858 Camp Walbach is established in what is now Laramie County.

September 21

1909 Municipal natural gas service starts in Basin.

September 22

1934 The self-declared "World Famous" Wonder Bar opens in Casper.

1937 A forest fire near Cody kills fourteen and injures fifty.

September 23

1897 Cheyenne Frontier Days is held for the first time.

September 24

1911 Governor Richards's daughter and son-in-law are murdered at Richards's Red Banks ranch on the Nowood.

September 25

1933 A memorial to June Downey, an important early professor with widely varying interests, is unveiled at the University of Wyoming. In addition to writing poetry, teaching English and, later, psychology and being a department head, she wrote the school's alma mater.

September 26

1872 Part of the Wind River Reservation is ceded to the United States.

1876 Additional Wind River Reservation lands are ceded to the United States.

1916 The Wyoming National Guard leaves for service on the Mexican border. It had been federalized during the summer.

September 27

1886 The cornerstone of Old Main is placed at the University of Wyoming.

1923 Thirty railroad passengers are killed when a Chicago, Burlington & Quincy (CB&Q) train wrecks at the Cole Creek Bridge, which had been washed out due to a flood, in Natrona County.

1954 The 300th AFA is returned to state control, although the Wyoming Guardsmen had mostly returned quite some time earlier, having served their full tours of duty.

September 28

1901 At Balangiga on Samar Island, Philippine villagers surprise the U.S. military Company C, Ninth Infantry Regiment. Of 74 U.S. soldiers, 38 were killed and all the rest but 6 were wounded. Philippine casualties were estimated at 50 to 250. Church bells, allegedly used to signal the attack, were taken by the Americans as prizes. Upon the Ninth Infantry's return, the bells were installed at Fort D.A. Russell, where they remain today at what is now F.E. Warren AFB. The Philippines still seeks their return, and the presence of the bells remains an ongoing controversy. A few years ago, a member of the Wyoming Veterans Commission lost his seat by stating that he supported their return. The Filipino representatives maintain that the bells in some cases reflect that they were taken from churches other than those near the battle.

1916 Two battalions of the Wyoming National Guard leave for the Mexican border.

September 29

1882 Fort Sanders, south of Laramie, is sold at public auction.

September 30

1889 The Constitutional Convention adopts the Wyoming constitution. This constitution, with amendments, remains in effect, which is unusual for state constitutions. Unlike the U.S. Constitution, state constitutions have tended to be replaced over time fairly frequently.

OCTOBER IN WYOMING

October is generally a pleasant month in Wyoming, but it can have some significant storms. It's a fall month, but the warning of the impending winter is there. For ranchers, those who have not trailed down from the high country now will. Cattle shipping is a major feature of the month.

October 1

1886 A total of 242 town lots are sold in Douglas.

October 2

1919 President Woodrow Wilson suffers a stroke that leaves him partially paralyzed. He had only recently been in Cheyenne.

1924 Governor William B. Ross dies while in office. His wife, Nellie Tayloe Ross, would become the United States' first female governor the month after she won a special election in spite of not campaigning. She would serve only until 1926, however, when she would lose a subsequent election.

1998 Major General Dennis K. Jackson becomes chief of ordnance for the army. He is a University of Wyoming graduate.

October 3

1866 The Regular Army arrives at Fort Caspar with troops from Company E, Second U.S. Cavalry, arriving as reinforcements.

1890 The U.S. secretary of the interior approves the sum of $20,000 for the surveying of public lands in Wyoming.

1895 Uinta County sheriff John Ward arrests Bannock Indian Race Horse for "the unlawful and wanton killing of seven elk in said county on the first day of July, 1895." Race Horse was exonerated when the United States Circuit Court held that the "provisions of the state statute were inconsistent with the treaty" of July 3, 1868.

October 4

1889 Bids are requested for the construction of a public school in Casper.

1909 Upton votes for incorporation.

October 5

1911 President William H. Taft addresses an audience at Rock Springs.

October 6

1890 The army abandons Fort Bridger.

1955 United Airlines Flight 409 crashes into Medicine Bow Peak, killing all sixty-six on board.

October 7

1857 Fort Bridger is torched by Mormon forces during the Mormon War.

1885 Those arrested for the Rock Springs riots are released.

1935 United Airlines Trip 4 crashes outside Cheyenne, killing all twelve persons on board.

1998 Matthew Shepard is found beaten, burned and tied to a wooden fence outside Laramie. He died several days later. His murder by two young Laramie men became the most infamous killing in Wyoming since the 1970s.

October 8

1889 The brewery in Sheridan burns.

1915 The first oil well is drilled in the Elk Basin.

October 9

1892 A natural gas deposit is discovered near the brewery in Buffalo.

1919 The first fatal airplane crash in Wyoming's history occurs when Lieutenant Edwin Wales's plane crashes in a snowstorm west of Cheyenne.

October 10

1890 A mine explosion at Almy kills one.

1902 Tom Horn is tried for the murder of Willie Nickell.

October 11

1890 Wyoming's first state-elected officers take their offices.

1912 The film *Charge of the Light Brigade* premieres. The film contains scenes that were filmed at the Army/Army National Guard training range of Pole Mountain.

1914 Richard Daniels Jr., one of the child actors in the Our Gang series, is born in Rock Springs. Daniels would continue to act into his early adult years and remained popular with fans but ultimately intentionally dropped out of sight. He died at age fifty-five due to the effects of alcoholism.

October 12

1869 The first territorial legislature is convened.

1876 Cantonment Reno is established.

October 13

1869 Fort Sanders, Wyoming, harvests three hundred bushels of turnips.

I wonder why turnips? Why not potatoes or onions? Turnips?

October 14

1963 The state penitentiary's Shaw High School graduates its first class.

October 15

1887 Mail service is discontinued between South Pass City and Lander.

1962 Construction firm Morrison-Knudsen wins a contract to construct two hundred Minuteman silos over an 8,300-square-mile area of Wyoming, Nebraska and Colorado.

1966 Bighorn Canyon National Recreation Area is established by Congress.

1984 Queen Elizabeth II visits her cousins, the Wallops, on their ranch in Sheridan.

October 16

1889 Emma Howell Knight, future dean of women at the University of Wyoming, and Wilbur Clinton Knight, future UW professor of mining and metallurgy, marry in Omaha, Nebraska. They were the future parents of legendary UW geology professor Samuel Howell "Doc" Knight.

1912 Clifford Hansen is born in Zenith, Wyoming. The Teton County rancher was governor from 1963 to 1967 and then senator from 1967 to 1978.

1916 The cavalry is withdrawn from Yellowstone National Park.

October 17

1937 The University of Wyoming Board of Trustees approves the contract for construction of the student union.

1945 An eleven-year-old girl shoots a seven-hundred-pound bear with a .22 near Worland.

1969 One of the most memorable events in Wyoming sports and social history occurs when all fourteen black players on the 1969 University of Wyoming football team walk into head coach Lloyd Eaton's office wearing black armbands. They hoped to convince Eaton to let them wear the armbands the following day in UW's football game against BYU to protest the Mormon Church's policy against blacks in the Mormon priesthood. Eaton dismissed them all from the team. The team was undefeated at the time.

The fourteen's actions put the university in a terrible spot, as the football team was among the best ever fielded by the University of Wyoming, and Eaton's actions effectively gutted the team. However, Easton felt that he could not allow the team to be used as a vehicle for protest. The entire matter ended up in a meeting the following day in which the governor met with the fourteen and the board of trustees of the university. In the end, no solution could be found, and the fourteen stuck to their position, Eaton remained coach and the board of trustees voted to support Eaton.

The entire matter ended up in litigation, which is not surprising. What is surprising, however, is that Judge Kerr, the federal judge presiding over the matter, initiated an effort to have the players and the coach meet on November 10, 1969, at the courthouse. Coach Eaton agreed, but the players did not take him up on this, and there was an objection to the suggestion by their attorney, who felt that a meeting would be a poor idea due to Eaton's strong personality. At least a couple players later indicated that they were aware that the offer to meet had been made. The case, therefore, proceeded into litigation, effectively dooming any chance of an immediate resolution.

The federal suit went up to the Tenth Circuit Court of Appeals twice. The entire matter was fought out after the fortunes of the football team that year had been sealed by the event.

1973 Arab oil-producing nations announce they will cut back oil exports to western nations and Japan, resulting in the Oil Embargo.

October 18

1868 Vigilantes hang three members of the Asa Moore Gang in Bosler, where some of the gang members owned a bar. One of the gang members, Big Steve Long, asked to leave his boots on, stating, "My mother always said I'd die with my boots on." He was lynched with his boots off.

1919 Robert Russin's statue of Lincoln on the interstate highway between Laramie and Cheyenne is dedicated. That route was part of the Lincoln Highway at the time, hence the dedication.

October 19

1867 Fort Caspar, Wyoming, is abandoned. It would be subsequently burned by the Indians.

1890 Troop A, First Cavalry Regiment, is relieved from assignment to Yellowstone National Park. The army patrolled the park until 1915.

1944 A bomber from the Casper Air Base crashes, killing three crew members.

October 20

1803 The Louisiana Purchase is ratified.

1906 Southeast Wyoming is hit by a three-day blizzard.

1958 Northeast Wyoming and southeast Montana are hit by a severe blizzard.

October 21

1803 The Senate authorizes President Jefferson to take possession of the Louisiana Territory and establish a temporary military government for the territory.

1866 Fort Philip Kearny is completed.

1872 Construction at the territorial prison in Laramie is completed.

1909 The cornerstone for Jireh College in Jireh is laid. Jireh College was a Protestant college that no longer exists. The town likewise no longer exists. Its history was relatively short, but it featured a combined effort to create a Christian school with a farming community.

October 22

1812 Robert Stuart and a small party of Astorians cross South Pass, making them the first Euro-Americans to do so.

October 23

1972 Fossil Butte National Monument is created.

October 24

1859 Residents of what are now parts of Colorado, Wyoming, Nebraska and Kansas vote to form the Territory of Jefferson. The extralegal putative territory would have included some of Wyoming but also would have included parts of what are now the neighboring states, including nearly all of Colorado. It was never afforded recognition by the United States, although, amazingly, it did elect a government and legislature. Admission of Kansas and, more particularly, Colorado into the Union ended it.

1861 The Pony Express is terminated.

Contrary to widespread popular belief, the riders weren't all orphans. Nor were they all young, as at least one rider was in his forties. The hard-riding part, however, is accurate.

1902 A jury, having gone out the day before for deliberation, finds Tom Horn guilty of the murder of Willie Nickell.

October 25

1906 Lovell is incorporated.

1923 The Teapot Dome scandal comes to public attention as Senator Thomas J. Walsh of Montana, subcommittee chairman, reveals the findings of the previous eighteen months of investigation.

October 26

1865 Companies A, C, F and G of the Sixth West Virginia Volunteer Cavalry arrive at Platte Bridge Station, Wyoming. They were certainly very far from home.

1880 The Cheyenne Club is incorporated.

1976 Yellowstone National Park is designated an International Biosphere Reserve.

2010 It is reported that Wyoming mystery writer C.J. Box donated his papers to the University of Wyoming.

October 27

1862 Captain Peter Van Winkle, Sixth Ohio Volunteer Cavalry, reports that he had twenty-eight men on station, had completed quarters and had completed construction of a stable at Platte Bridge Station. The location was not an entirely new one, as it was the location of Guinards Bridge on the Oregon Trail and had periodically been occupied by the army previously. His construction efforts, which essentially completed the original post, were new, however. He also reported that he had sufficient stores of food to last until April, although the size of his command would double by the end of the week.

1867 Troops from Fort D.A. Russell destroy squatters' shanties on the Union Pacific line near Cheyenne.

1933 Ernest Hemingway's collection of short stories *Winner Take Nothing*, including "Wine of Wyoming," is published.

October 28

1919 The Volstead Act goes into effect. Booze—banned.

Wyoming senator F.E. Warren was instrumental in the passage of the Volstead Act, which he supported, having cast the deciding vote in its passage.

1926 The Buffalo Bill Museum in Cody is formed.

October 29

1917 Record cold strikes the West, with Soda Butte, Wyoming's temperature falling to negative thirty-three degrees Fahrenheit, a U.S. record for October. Lander's temperature fell to negative fourteen degrees and Cheyenne's to two degrees.

1943 The National Housing Agency approves one hundred trailers for Casper for essential immigrant war workers.

October 30

1866 A grand pass and review is held at recently established, and semi-besieged, Fort Phil Kearny.

1889 CB&Q Railroad enters Wyoming.

1913 A superior approves an ordinance declaring animals and livestock at large to be a nuisance.

1959 Wyoming's fourth uranium mill begins production in the Gas Hills.

October 31—Halloween

1945 Wyoming Game and Fish agents Bill Lakanen and Don Simpson are shot and killed while responding to a report of poaching in the Rawlins, Wyoming area. They are two of five Wyoming Game and Fish employees to be killed in the line of duty. Their case is particularly unique, as there was at least a suspicion that their killer, a native German, was known to be sympathetic with recently defeated Nazi Germany, and there had been some earlier reports of interior radio traffic in the general region (a very broad area) directed toward German receipt regarding the weather, a fact useful to submarines. This, however, was not proven to amount to anything, and the FBI did not track down the source of the alleged broadcast. The suspected killer was never found but was believed to be inside a cabin located where the game wardens were killed.

NOVEMBER IN WYOMING

Sidebar: Elections and History in Wyoming

November is election season, so some note of the history of politics in Wyoming is warranted. What does the history of Wyoming's voting show us? It's commonly asserted that Wyoming, which is now a solidly Republican state, always has been. That's partially true, but voting results show that doesn't mean quite what it might seem to, and also, beyond that, being in the Republican Party in early years didn't mean quite what it might seem to.

Wyoming obtained statehood in 1890. That year was still well within the influence of the Civil War, and that continued to have an impact on politics at that time and for about a decade after. The fortunes of the Republican Party had been somewhat solidified as a result of the war, but that was also true for the Democrats. In a way, what secession had attempted was reflected in the popularity of the political parties. The GOP was very strong in the North, and the Democratic Party dominated the South. States in the Midwest tended to be in a state of flux. In the West—where most of the territory was just that, territory—the GOP was by far the stronger party as a rule.

The GOP of the 1860s had a strong liberal element in it, which was particularly reflective of its antislavery policy of 1860–65. That part of the party had grown in strength during the war, and by the end of the war, Radical Republicans, who favored a harsh Reconstruction designed to immediately address racial issues in the South, were a strong element. They never took control of it, however. The party also was pro-business and was in favor of governmental assistance to business when it seemed merited. The best example of that is probably the Transcontinental Railroad, which was backed by the federal government and was a massive expenditure in various ways. That wasn't the only example, however. The Homestead Act, which gave away federal property that had formerly been held until turned over completely to newly admitted states, created an official policy of bribing migrants with offers of land from the federal stock of the same. The Homestead Act was a Republican act. The Mining Law of 1872, which worked in a similar fashion, likewise was a Republican act.

President U.S. Grant. *Library of Congress.*

The Democrats, in contrast, were more of a conservative party in some ways, although again the distinction cannot be directly carried into modern times. Democrats tended to favor individual states' rights more than Republicans did. For that reason, Democrats had generally opposed the Union effort during the Civil War, no matter where they lived.

A huge difference between the parties at that time was that the GOP had a legacy of freeing the slaves and the Democrats had effectively been the party of slavery. After the war, for that reason, the Democrats remained extremely strong in the South, where they continued to promote policies that were racist in nature. The GOP drew the support of recently freed slaves, but it was moderate in its attempts to assist them.

Given the war, the fortunes of the Democratic Party were very bleak at first following it, but perhaps somewhat surprisingly, they recovered more quickly than generally imagined. Democrats were contending seriously for national office much more rapidly than expected. Underlying all this, however, is the fact that there were serious rifts in both parties that would start to dramatically emerge in the 1890s, particularly after the Panic of 1893 threw the country into a truly massive depression.

The Democratic Party at the time was not a naturally unified party in part because it had such a strong southern base. The South had been divided before the war into a patrician class and a yeoman class that did not see eye to eye on many things, and after the war, this divide turned into a canyon. The patrician class, in a dedicated effort to restore as many of its prewar privileges as possible, operated against the rights of the yeomanry, which colossally resented it. Southern white yeomanry, all rural and agricultural, lost ground in terms of rights after Reconstruction, and only ongoing racial prejudice kept them from joining blacks in the Republican Party, which would have virtually destroyed the Democratic Party in the country overnight. They remained Democrats, however, as they could not see themselves joining a party they associated with blacks and the Union cause in the Civil War. What this did mean, however, is that a large number of southern Democrats were really something else.

This also started to be true in the GOP. After the war, the radical elements of the GOP felt increasingly frustrated by the inability to bring about a radical restructuring of the nation. Nearly a century ahead of themselves in some ways, their frustration, in some instances, grew into an increasing reformist drive.

Wyoming entered the political scene, of course, with the election of 1890. At that time, it entered into statehood with a dominant Republican structure. But voting trends reveal that many average Wyomingites had decamped, or were about to, into the more radical branches of politics.

Wyoming's first delegates to Washington were solidly Republican. The state elected the now-forgotten Republican Clarence D. Clark to the House of Representatives. Senators were appointed, not elected at the time, but the Republican legislature sent two giants of Wyoming's early history, Francis E. Warren and Joseph M. Carey, to the Senate. It would be tempting to believe that Wyoming has sent Republicans ever since, but this simply isn't true.

Senator Warren late in life but still wearing the Medal of Honor he won during the Civil War. Warren survived an early vague association with the Johnson County invaders and went on to have an extremely long political career. *Library of Congress.*

Indeed, in 1892, Wyoming already acted to put a Democrat into the House, Sheridan lawyer Henry A. Coffeen, for whom Coffeen Avenue in Sheridan is named. Coffeen served only a single term, but clearly something was already afoot that was upsetting Wyoming voters. Moreover, voters tossed out Republican governor Barber that year and installed Democratic governor Osborne, although Barber actually tried to physically retain his office by locking himself in it—not a very dignified end to his term.

What was going on in 1892? Well, simply the Johnson County War.

The Johnson County War seriously tainted the GOP in Wyoming, as it was so strongly associated with it. The GOP controlled the legislature and had sent all the delegates to Washington, and it was fairly clear that many significant Republicans in office knew of the plan to invade Johnson County. Suddenly associated with "big" moneyed interest, and as opponents of small ranchers and seemingly willing to endorse extra-legal violent action, it took a pounding in the elections and lost the legislature, the governor's office and even the position of congressman. At least Senator Warren was worried for a time that he might lose his position due to the Johnson County War.

None of that can solidly be attributed to a national trend, and it didn't last long. The GOP did regain control of the offices it lost fairly quickly, but it came at a time when populism was up and coming in both the GOP and the Democratic Party nationally. This is often missed in terms of discussions on Wyoming's politics. The election of 1892 might not have been just the voters' attempt to punish the state GOP; it may also have reflected the growing influence of populism in the United States in general. The Republican Party in Wyoming was not Populist. The Democratic Party and a third party that was allied to it that year were.

This would help explain the results of the presidential election in Wyoming of the same year. In that year, pro-business Bourbon Democrat Grover

Populist candidate James B. Weaver. *Library of Congress.*

Cleveland became the only president to regain office after having previously lost a bid for reelection. Cleveland was a candidate whom those leaning Republican could generally support, which explains in part how his political fortunes revived, but he did not gain support in Wyoming. In Wyoming, as we will see in a later entry, the state's electorate, which was voting for representatives to the Electoral College for the first time, given its recent statehood, went for Populist James Weaver. The general election of 1892 saw four candidates compete for electoral votes. In Wyoming, President Harrison ended up polling just over 50 percent, with Populist James Weaver taking 46 percent of the Wyoming vote. The remaining percentage of the vote seemingly went to John Bidwell of the Prohibition Party. Cleveland's percentage of the Wyoming vote was infinitesimal.

As surprising as this is, Wyoming was not unique in this regard. Weaver polled so well in Colorado that he pulled out ahead of Harrison in that state and took that state's electoral votes. He also won in Idaho, Nevada and North Dakota. Cleveland was obviously very unpopular in the Rocky Mountain West in the 1892 election. Indeed, Cleveland only took California and Texas in the West and polled most strongly in the East and the South. He polled particularly well in the Deep South that year, although Weaver also did well in the South. Cleveland's status as a Democrat probably carried him in the South.

This probably is an interesting comment on both the evolution of political parties and the makeup of the Wyoming electorate at the time. Wyoming remained a Republican state then as now, but at that time, the Republican Party had started to split between "progressive" and "conservative" factions. While its fiscal policies significantly differed in general, the Democratic Party had not yet started to have a significant populist branch, but it was already the case that its northern candidates, like Cleveland, were more easily recognizable to northern Republican voters than were southern Democrats. While Weaver didn't take any southern state, he did receive a large number of votes in the Deep South,

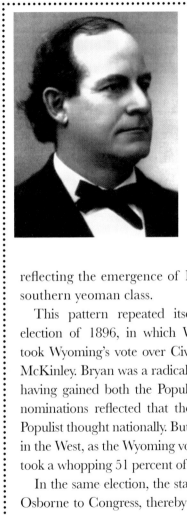

William Jennings Bryan.
Library of Congress.

reflecting the emergence of Populist thought in the southern yeoman class.

This pattern repeated itself in the presidential election of 1896, in which William Jennings Bryan took Wyoming's vote over Civil War veteran William McKinley. Bryan was a radical by all accounts, and his having gained both the Populist and the Democratic nominations reflected that the parties had swung to Populist thought nationally. But Bryan was also popular in the West, as the Wyoming vote demonstrated. Bryan took a whopping 51 percent of the Wyoming vote.

In the same election, the state sent former governor Osborne to Congress, thereby electing a Democrat to the House of Representatives. Seemingly, this reflected a Populist streak of some sort that extended to all federal candidates in Wyoming that year. The state returned a Republican to the governor's office, however, in 1894, so the trend was hardly universal. And long-serving, if generally forgotten, Clarence D. Clark remained in office throughout this period.

The next presidential election would see Theodore Roosevelt run for office, and he was a very popular candidate in the West. He was also from the

Theodore Roosevelt. *Library of Congress.*

progressive branch of the Republican Party, so any Populist elements that were headed toward being Democratic were effectively cut off.

With Republican fortunes gained during the Theodore Roosevelt administration and when his handpicked successor, Vice President William Howard Taft, ran in 1908, Wyoming demonstrated that it had lost its fondness for William Jennings Bryan, who ran against him. Taft took 55 percent of the Wyoming vote. Perhaps reflecting some residual racialism or perhaps due to the recent increase in immigration from Eastern Europe in some counties, Socialist candidate Eugene Debs amazingly took 4.5 percent of the vote. Statewide, Wyomingites seemed satisfied with Republican candidates once again.

Taft had the misfortune of following Roosevelt, who was a great man but still a young man, in relative terms, and just couldn't avoid politics. Taft basically acted as a reformist candidate, but a somewhat moderate one, and Roosevelt, for his part, was becoming increasingly radical. By the election of 1912, the split in the Republican Party that this represented broke the party apart, and after Taft was nominated, it actually became two parties, with the Rooseveltians becoming the Progressive Party. The Progressive Party would be a radical party even by today's standards, and it says something about the politics of the time that it mounted a very serious campaign and had nationwide support. At the same time, the Democrats began to tack toward the Progressives themselves and pick up parts of their platform. The transformation of the Democratic Party into a liberal party really began with the presidential election of 1912, and by the end of the election, the party was never again quite what it had been, although the change would continue on for years thereafter.

Woodrow Wilson took Wyoming's electoral vote that year, receiving 42 percent of the popular vote. The combined Taft and Roosevelt vote surpassed that, with Roosevelt taking 27 percent of the vote, a greater share than that taken by Taft. Socialist Eugene Debs came in with an amazing 6 percent. Given this, it is not possible to simply write off the election to the split in the Republican Party that year. The combined Debs and Roosevelt vote made up a whopping 33 percent of the Wyoming electorate that was expressing support for a radical change in direction in national politics. Wilson's 42 percent was not insignificant either. Even simply writing off the fact that any Democratic candidate of that era would have received at least one-third of the state vote, a surprising number of Wyomingites seemed to be espousing the progressive, and even radical, ideas that were the

Woodrow Wilson. *Library of Congress.*

combined platforms of the Progressive and Democratic Parties. Even accepting that the Democrats had come at this development through the Populists, which was reflected in their earlier nomination of Bryan and in Wilson's appointing him to the position of secretary of state, it seems something was afoot.

Indeed, in the same year, the sitting governor elected in 1910, Joseph M. Carey, left the Republican Party and joined the Progressive Party. Carey, like most (but not all) of the Progressives, including Theodore Roosevelt himself, would eventually return to the Republican Party, but it's at least interesting to note that a sitting, elected Wyoming governor publicly abandoned his party to join a third party. A thing like that would simply be inconceivable today.

This trend, moreover, continued. Carey's successor in the governor's office was not a member of the Republican Party or a Progressive but Democrat

John B. Kendrick. Kendrick did not remain in that office for long, however, as he was elected to the United States Senate by the electorate, which was now able to directly elect senators, in 1916, a position he held until his death in 1933. His companion in the Senate for most of that time, however, was very long-serving Republican

Senator John B. Kendrick. *Library of Congress.*

senator Francis E. Warren (who, of course, had also been a governor), who served until his death in 1929, when he was replaced by Republican senator Patrick Sullivan.

A slow shift began to take place in the early teens, however. In the 1916 presidential election, the state again supported Wilson, giving him 49 percent of the vote. An additional 3 percent supported Socialist candidate Allan Benson, and those votes would certainly have gone for any more left wing candidate than Republican Charles Hughes, but a period in which Wyoming leaned Republican but would swing toward Democrat was emerging. The state went very strongly for Warren Harding in 1920 (60 percent) and for Coolidge in 1924. In 1924, however, the Democrats fared very poorly in the presidential election, with the Progressive candidate, Robert LaFollette—who had taken up where Theodore Roosevelt would not have wanted to leave off for him and then some—receiving 31 percent of the Wyoming vote. David, the Democrat, came in a poor third, showing that a strong Progressive streak remained in the Wyoming electorate at that time. That election saw the nation nearly completely go for Coolidge except in the South, which went for Davis. Geographically, it was one of the most divided elections in the nation's history.

In 1928, the state went for Hoover. In 1932, however, like the rest of the nation, it went for Franklin Roosevelt, who took every single state in the Union that year. In 1936, it went for FDR by an even higher margin, and it would go for FDR again in 1940 and 1944. In 1948, it went for Truman.

Other offices, however, present a less clear story. Francis E. Warren and John B. Kendrick both died in office and were succeeded by members of their party, a legal requirement. But those seats remained safely in those parties up until the Great Depression saw both Senate seats occupied briefly by Democrats, when Henry Schwartz was elected for a single term. After Democratic Schwartz lost his seat in 1940, it returned to Republican control until 1948, when the tragic figure of Lester Hunt occupied it. At that point, once again, both Senate positions were occupied by Democrats for a time.

The story was similar in the U.S. House of Representatives. Republicans generally dominated that position for Wyoming, but in the midst of the Great Depression and World War II, Democrats briefly occupied it. Those periods, however, were brief and seem to have indicated voter upset about the Depression itself and, later, voter favor over Democratic control of the war effort.

The governor's office, however, seems to reveal something else. The position proved to be extremely volatile and competitive between the parties, and contrary to the Wyoming myth, many Democrats occupied it. It shifted back and forth between the parties constantly after the 1918 election of Republican Robert D. Carey. Looking at the shift between the parties would almost seem to indicate that the voters liked both or grew rapidly dissatisfied with either. No stability in party occupation of the office existed at all until the 1950s, when the

Republicans occupied the governor's office for a decade.

Attempting to define eras, let alone political eras, is always a risky endeavor. But in Wyoming's case, it does seem to be the situation that the politics of the state began to change after World War II. For the first few decades after the war, Democrats continued to be able to contend in Wyoming for state and federal offices, but starting in the mid-1970s, that began to end. The state supported Harry Truman in his 1948 reelection bid and again supported Lyndon Johnson in his 1964 campaign, but it did not support the generally popular John F. Kennedy in his 1960 campaign, and it never supported a Democratic candidate for the presidency after Lyndon Johnson. As late as the 1970s, the state continued to elect Democrats to both houses of Congress, with Teno Roncolio and Gale McGee both serving Wyoming in that decade, but after they left office, they were replaced by Republicans, and the GOP has held all the congressional positions since that time.

The exception to the rule seems to be the governor's office, where Democrats have remained contenders up to the present day. Ed Herschler was elected governor an unprecedented three times, serving into the 1980s. Mike Sullivan proved to be a popular two-term Democratic governor following Republican governor Geringer.

Sullivan, in turn, was followed by Dave Freudenthal, another Democrat who served two terms, who was followed by Republican Matt Mead. Perhaps signaling that the governor's office remains somewhat unique, Governor Mead is generally regarded as a middle-of-the-road Republican, just as it was often claimed that Sullivan and Freudenthal would have been Republicans in any other state. The governor's office, for the most part, has tended to attract candidates who are quite independent, and it's notable that the governor generally enjoys respect from the overwhelmingly Republican legislature no matter what party he is from, even though both Republican and Democratic governors have frequently disagreed with the legislature on many things.

Be that as it may, save for the governor's office, the period following the 1970s has been overwhelmingly Republican in Wyoming, and the fortunes of the Democratic Party have enormously declined. Why is that the case? This is hard to say, and there are no doubt a million theories, but one thing that is commonly noted is that national candidates drew increasingly less support in Wyoming following LBJ. And it cannot be denied that both the GOP and the Democratic Party changed in the 1960s. The Democrats who remained popular in Wyoming in the 1970s had their roots in an earlier Democratic Party, and those who have run since the 1970s tended to distance themselves from the national party. The Democrats have come to be seen as an increasingly urban party, and the party's support for things such as gun control has been very unpopular with Wyoming voters and has required the local party to attempt to separate itself from the national party. This trend isn't unique to Wyoming, and many commentators have noted that the parties have become increasingly polarized in recent decades. Wyoming became very hostile territory for Democrats during the Clinton administration, and the decline in success of the party became quite pronounced from that point forward.

At any rate, the history of Wyoming politics is interesting in these regards, as what that history tends to show is that Wyoming's voters have been highly independent over the decades rather than completely reliable for any one party. In its early decades, the state flirted with progressivism and populism. In the middle decades of the twentieth century, it doesn't seem to have been reliable for any party. After World War II, it became increasingly Republican territory, and this particularly became the case after the 1960s. As politics is history, in a very real sense, this history is worth noting in any book that attempts to catalogue the history of the state.

November 1

1886 The first snowfall of what would prove to be a disastrous winter.

1911 The Wyoming General Hospital opens in Casper. The hospital remains open today, in different quarters, as the Wyoming Medical Center.

1919 A contingent of the Fifteenth Cavalry under the command of Major Warren Dean arrives at Fort Mackenzie from Fort D.A. Russell in order to deal with labor strife at Carneyville, near Sheridan.

1940 The 115th Cavalry Regiment, Wyoming National Guard, is redesignated the 115th Cavalry Regiment (Horse Mechanized). The change in designation came about as a reflection in a de facto change in the unit, which was made into a new category in the army. Horse mechanized was a late cavalry-era effort to incorporate motorization within the horse-mounted units. While no horse mechanized unit ever saw action in the U.S. Army during World War II, the concept was not far from what was actually employed by the Soviet Union during the war.

The 115th Cavalry had a very good reputation early in its mobilization period and was highly praised by Lucien

Truscott, the World War II general, in his book *Twilight of the Cavalry*.

1943 The War Housing Administration meets with residents of Green River about upcoming housing projects.

November 2

1812 Robert Stuart and five others begin construction of a cabin at the mouth of the Poison Spider Creek in Natrona County. The cabin was the first known to be built by European Americans in Wyoming, although this does not discount the possibility that French Canadian trappers might have built structures earlier.

The cabin proved to be very temporary, as it happened to be built in an area of inter-tribal Indian strife and, therefore, was a dangerous location. Smith and company soon pulled up stakes and relocated for the winter in the location of the current Scotsbluff, Nebraska.

For many years, this cabin was marked by a Wyoming Historical Marker sign noting it as the "First White Man's Cabin in Wyoming," but the sign came down some twenty years ago and was never put back up.

November 3

1762 Spain acquires Louisiana from France. As of this date, a small part of Wyoming that was previously French Louisiana was Spanish Louisiana. But not for long.

1890 The U.S. District Court for the District of Wyoming goes into session for the first time.

1999 Aaron McKinney is convicted of the murder of Matthew Shepard the year prior.

November 4

1804 Lewis and Clark record in their journal that Sacagawea was the wife of Toussaint Charbonneau. In fact, she was one of two wives whom Charbonneau had married either at the same time or close in time, with both of them being in their mid-teens at the time. He'd marry three more times during his life, with his last marriage coming at age seventy. All of his wives were Native Americans, and none of them was older than sixteen at the time of the marriage.

1856 The Mormon Martin's Handcart Company, attempting a late crossing of the Oregon Trail and having run into trouble with the weather, seeks shelter in the Martin's Cove area near Independence Rock, along with a rescue party that was sent to find them. They had not embarked on their efforts until August 27, making an attempt to cross extraordinary late in the year.

1889 A meeting regarding the ratification of Wyoming's constitution is held in Rawlins.

1924 Nellie Tayloe Ross of Wyoming is elected the nation's first female governor in a special election to fill the term of her late husband, who had been governor. She would serve until 1927, when she would leave office after having narrowly lost the 1926 election. She refused to campaign in either election but remained popular nonetheless. Her 1926 loss is likely attributable to her refusal to campaign, which her opponent did, and her strong support for Prohibition. She would later serve in Franklin Roosevelt's administration and in Truman's administration as the head of the United States Mint.

November 5

1879 The U.S. Army establishes camp on the Snake River.

1889 Wyoming's constitution is approved by the electorate.

1943 A United States Army Air Corps bomber crashes near Evanston.

November 6

1889 Wyoming's constitution is adopted. The Wyoming constitution is unusual for a state constitution in that it has survived, albeit with amendments, since adoption. Most U.S. states have replaced their original state constitutions. The constitution was the first of a U.S. state to provide for female suffrage.

1890 The last troops stationed at Fort Bridger depart.

1900 A terrible train wreck occurs near Tie Siding in Albany County.

1908 Robert LeRoy Parker, aka "Butch" Cassidy, and Harry Alonzo Lonabaugh, aka the "Sundance Kid," are killed in a gun battle with Bolivian cavalry in San Vincete, Bolivia. While Parker and Lonabaugh were regional criminals, they were headquartered in Johnson County's Hole in the Wall country for most of their U.S. criminal career.

1930 J.B. Okie, a giant in the sheep industry and a relocated wealthy easterner, dies while duck hunting near Lost Cabin, his Wyoming home. Okie's life reads somewhat like a soap opera. Economically, his small start in the sheep industry turned into a giant regional industry centered on Fremont and Natrona Counties, with a large headquarters in Lost Cabin, a railhead in Lysite and stores elsewhere.

J.B. Okie's mansion, the "Big Teepee" in Lost Cabin.
Photograph by the author.

Big Horn Sheep Company headquarters in Lost Cabin.
Photograph by the author.

1981 The U.S. Fish and Wildlife Service announces that a black-footed ferret, an animal presumed extinct, has been discovered in Wyoming.

November 7

1871 The second session of Wyoming's Territorial Legislative Assembly begins. It continued until December 16.

1877 The fifth session of Wyoming's Territorial Legislative Assembly begins.

November 8

1876 Mary Davis is elected justice of the peace in Tie Siding, Wyoming, a small town outside Laramie. She was the first woman in Wyoming to be elected to the position (there had been women appointed as justice of the peace previously).

1957 The Most Reverend Patrick A. McGovern, Catholic bishop of the Diocese of Cheyenne, dies after occupying his office for thirty-nine years. Bishop McGovern had been an orphan and grew up in Omaha, Nebraska. As bishop of the Diocese of Cheyenne, he was active in his concern for the plight of Wyoming's orphans.

November 9

1849 William "Red" Angus is born in Zanesville, Ohio. Angus would be employed as a teamster, drover and bar owner before ending up the sheriff of Johnson County in 1888. He was sheriff during the Johnson County War. He lost the election in 1893 and later went on to be the Johnson County treasurer. He died in 1920 and is buried in Buffalo.

1856 Warming weather allows the Martin Handcart Company to resume traveling on the Oregon Trail.

1867 John Hardy and John Shaughnessy compete in a prizefight in Cheyenne.

1883 The Wyoming Stock Growers Association meets in Cheyenne to discuss problems with branding iron usage and roundup irregularities. The meeting would result in a blacklist of disapproved brands and operators.

1894 Fort McKinney is abandoned by the army.

1902 Two female justices of the peace are elected in Laramie County.

November 10

1945 Heart Mountain internment center is closed.

1969 Judge Ewing T. Kerr hears testimony in the action brought in support of the Black 14. The court takes the matter under advisement.

1997 The Wyoming Air National Guard commences operations in Operation Tempest Rapid No. 1, a firefighting mission to Indonesia. Flying until December 5, the unit would fly 250 missions in the U.S. Air Force's first overseas firefighting mission.

November 11—Veterans Day

1865 The U.S. Army renames Fort Connor to Fort Reno in honor of Major General Jesse L. Reno.

1890 The Wyoming Supreme Court meets for the first time.

1918 World War I comes to an end in an armistice.

1943 The commander of the prisoner of war camp in Douglas announces that one thousand Italians held at the camp will be helping with the fall harvest. Given the timing of the announcement, it would have to be presumed that the harvest was well underway at the time. As Douglas itself is not in a farming belt, it would be interesting to know where the POWs actually went and how they were housed.

Sidebar:
Wyoming and World War I

Except for the particularly historically minded, World War I seems pretty remote in time. It's no wonder, really, as the war was overshadowed in the American imagination (but not the European one) a mere twenty or so years after it ended by World War II, which to Americans has always seemed the much more critical and bigger event. Indeed, to the American imagination, World War I often seems to be not much more than the prologue to World War II.

And, of course, World War II defines modern wars. Every war that's happened since can find some precedent in World War II, and even though technology has enormously advanced since the war, up until extremely recently there's always been a close precedent in any one weapon or ground environment in a current war and the Second World War. Perhaps this is changing just now, in which case, I suppose, World War II will soon seem to be a much more distant war. World War I managed to seem distant, somehow, to Americans by 1939, when the Germans invaded Poland.

World War I was actually a much more modern war than we now imagine. And in actuality, during the war itself, the impact of World War I in the state may have exceeded that of World War II; the long-lasting impacts may in fact be less obvious but potentially greater. Much of what Wyoming is today it became in the twentieth century, and even if it started to become what it is today in the late nineteenth century, the big changes really started during World War I.

The Great War, for Wyoming, started in 1914 when the Germans entered Belgium. The same is not true, at least to the same extent, of 1939, when the Germans entered Poland, or even of 1940, when the Germans entered Belgium again. The reason for this has to do with two prime resources that Wyoming had at that time that were vital to the European war: the horse and petroleum oil.

When the war broke out, British Remount agents scoured the United States for suitable horses of all types. Wyoming was ideally situated to take advantage of this sudden boom in the requirements for horseflesh. Northern Wyoming and Montana, which had significant English ranching communities, were particularly eager to take part in this trade, which not only provided a readymade market for fine horses but also appealed to their English patriotism. But they were not alone in taking advantage of this market. Range horses—that is, horses simply gathered off the range—had long been a staple for ranchers, but now they actually commanded the attention of foreign purchasers. The horse boom was on.

British Remount purchasing agents were joined by French purchasing agents seeking to do the same thing. Wyoming, of course, wasn't unique in its ability to provide horses, but with thousands of available horses and some fine independent breeding programs, the economic impact of European purchases was vast.

The boom in this agricultural commodity, however, was not isolated. Every sector of agriculture in North America exploded during the Great War. From 1914 on, the fields of France were strained by fighting and a lack of war workers. The UK was free of fighting, of course, but it was also free of agricultural workers, as they joined the British army to fight in the war. And both of these factors were also true for Russia, a major grain-producing region. Every place where grain could be planted, and many places that never should have had grain planted, received it.

Of course, the need to feed a vast number of men also increased the demand for meat and, therefore, cattle. Sheep also saw a boom. This was in the height of Wyoming's sheep era, when sheep numbered in the millions in the state. The armies of Europe fought in wool, and the demand for wool was inexhaustible.

This all started in the 1914 to 1917 time frame, before the United States had entered the war. Wyoming was enjoying a war-related economic boom before the country entered. Starting in 1915, the war actually arrived in another form in Wyoming in the form of the Punitive Expedition, which is not commonly regarded as being part of World War I at all but was the country's introduction to the fighting in some ways. The Wyoming National Guard (there was no "Army" National Guard at the time, just the National Guard) saw itself federalized for service on the border just like every other state's guard. While service was not continual, the Punitive Expedition was the de facto start of the war for the United States Army, which began to expand at this point and began to receive practical field experience for the greater war that was to come. From this point until 1919, the army was at least partially mobilized and on a war footing.

Wyoming, at the time, was home to two army bases: Fort D.A. Russell and Fort MacKenzie. Both were horse-centric, as cavalry was stationed at Fort D.A. Russell and Fort MacKenzie was a remount purchasing center. Wyoming's National Guard was artillery at the time, for the most part, with some other types of units mixed in, but it did not include cavalry. Nonetheless, as is obvious, the United States soon also became a purchaser of horseflesh due to its military requirements. The horse boom, therefore, was compounded.

When war was declared in April 1917, the United States found itself dealing with the first draft since the Civil War. Indeed, due to an odd opinion by the attorney general of the United States, conscription actually applied to the federalized National Guardsmen. In a legal oddity, all the guardsmen were discharged and then instantly conscripted. But of course, they weren't alone. The United States Army expanded from a tiny force to one of more than one million men in next to no time. Absorbing the influx of men itself was a problem only partially solved by the army's solution of dividing itself into two groups, one part being the combined Regular Army and National Guard and the other, the National Army, being made up of conscripts. Ultimately, the National Army would outnumber the combined guard and Regular Army.

Like World War II, the Great War depleted towns of their entire young male populations. Young men were so eager to join that they actually crossed the state in some circumstances to volunteer. Young men from Jackson formed their own unit and traveled to Cheyenne to join, for example. As the Great War would be the death of private units, and these men were no doubt incorporated into another unit, they might have been a bit disappointed. Nonetheless, the extent of volunteerism was so high that even a relatively small town like Hanna left behind memorials to large numbers of men who volunteered to serve in the war.

The drain on agricultural workers was so high in this largely pre-mechanized agricultural era that the United States, like Britain and Canada before it, was forced to recruit women for labor in the fields.

The era of the war also saw the expansion of military training to schools, something that had not been common prior to the war. Casper High School, the predecessor to Natrona County High School, fielded an early version of Jr. ROTC. The University of Wyoming incorporated officer training. Officer training at universities was not invented in this era, but it was widespread during the war.

The swelling of the army naturally increased the demand on all the resources already being produced for the war in Wyoming. Grains, meat and wool all became even more in demand just as the labor to produce all of them became more scarce.

Food concerns became so acute, in fact, during the Great War that a major governmental campaign was launched seeking to conserve certain foods. This was also done, of course, during World War I, but the World War I effort had a certain desperate tinge to it. Indeed, the desperate tinge in World War I actually led to a rationing program in Montana, although there was not nationwide rationing as there was in World War II. Montana actually prosecuted some people under a state anti-sedition law for criticizing its rationing program.

One vital wartime commodity was petroleum oil. As with horses, oil experienced a boom starting in 1914. For the first time in history, armies were using oil in significant quantities as motor transportation made its appearance. Perhaps more significantly, however, the Royal Navy had started the switch in 1911 to burning oil rather than coal, even though the United Kingdom was entirely dependent on oil imports. The U.S. Navy had started this switch the year prior, in 1910. Wyoming had been an oil province since the late nineteenth century, and the war dramatically boosted production, causing a joint oil and agricultural boom in the state. Even prior to that, Congress, realizing that the switch to petroleum oil by the navy meant that war could create a shortfall of the strategic resource, had committed some of Wyoming's oil to a Strategic Petroleum Reserve for the U.S. Navy. This gave Wyoming, somewhat uniquely for a landlocked state, a navy presence prior to the war.

It was the oil boom that caused the most visible and perhaps the most long-lasting change to the state. With the expansion of oil exploration came the modernization and expansion of oil production facilities, as well as the explosive buildup of towns and cities. The state saw skyscrapers built during the war, such as Casper's Oil Exchange Building, which later became the Consolidated Royalty Building. Construction also included housing, streets and sidewalks as new urban areas were developed to house the workforce brought in by the expansion in oil production. In some ways, the long-developing position of the minerals industry as the prime economic mover of the state finally took permanent hold during World War I. Agriculture remained, of course, important, but there was no denying the greatly increased importance of oil production.

The war caused a shift, so dramatic that it must have been obvious to those living in the state at the time, from an economy and culture that was primarily focused on cattle ranching to one based on oil exploration. Wyoming had, of course, seen mineral exploration prior to 1914, and some Wyoming towns were entirely dedicated to it in some fashion. But the real intense exploration had been devoted mostly to coal, giving rise to towns like Hanna. Otherwise, even if they featured oil exploration as part of their economic base, most Wyoming towns were agricultural in some fashion. Casper, as an example, might have boosted its fortunes in newspapers as an oil center, but it was cattle and sheep that kept the town going. Starting in 1914, it really did become an oil town, even with the cattle and sheep remaining.

Just as the war sparked a huge economic boom in the state, the end of the war brought a responding crash. Agriculture hung on economically for about a year nationwide after the war ended, with 1919 being the last year in U.S. history in which the standard of living for a family farm met that for the average middle-class town dweller. But that same year, the expansion of grain production continued on unabated with near obvious results, and homesteading reached its all-time high. A crash was bound to follow. The reduction of armies globally and the cessation of the need for horses of course brought about an end to the remount trade in a big hurry, causing an immediate horse recession for those who had been supplying horses to the various Allied armies. While the Great Depression would not arrive for another decade, for agriculture, the slump started early all across the nation and would only grow worse in the 1930s. Nonetheless, at the same time, a last gasp of homesteading would continue on until it was stopped by the federal government in 1933.

Oddly enough, the war directly caused a brief burst of immediate postwar homesteading, with some being fairly successful, under a special program to assist returning servicemen in that fashion. The program was seemingly fairly popular with returning veterans. Perhaps reflecting a change in society, a similar program at the end of World War II was largely unsuccessful and underutilized.

Oil carried on as the economic engine of the state following the war after a slump, reflecting the enormous expansion of automobiles that had commenced the decade prior to the war and would continue on unabated until the Great Depression. Following World War I, and as a result of it, the army would experiment with cross-country road travel, giving a boost to the highway movement that was already ongoing. The United States began its real conversion to a highway society following the war, although certainly trains remained the dominant means of cross-country and even intrastate travel.

Just as the war may have given a boost to the travel of humans, it certainly gave a boost to the travel of disease, and Wyoming suffered, along with the rest of the nation, from the 1918 influenza epidemic that the war caused and spread. Calendar entries occasionally note the death toll from this horrific global event, which, while global, visited personalized grief on communities and individuals in the state that year.

In terms of social changes, or perhaps political ones, World War I did not have the massive impacts that World War II did, but it did have some. Perhaps the most surprising is the success of Prohibition. The movement toward Prohibition had been in the country since the late nineteenth century, but it was the war that caused the Volstead Act and the amendment to the U.S. Constitution, changes in which Wyoming had a role. Wyoming's politicians on a town and state level began agitating for Prohibition as soon as the United States entered the war. The mayor of Cheyenne, for example, urged it as a way of ensuring civil conduct in the town in light of the increased numbers of soldiers at Fort D.A. Russell. The governor asked for bars to be closed for the duration of the war. Politicians expressed a fear that soldiers would return from France drunks or worse after having sampled French wine and whatever other illicit offerings France might have in store. F.E. Warren, seeing which way the wind was blowing, provided the decisive vote in the Senate to push the Volstead Act over the top. Prohibition arrived in 1919 with the returning veterans, which was not an accident.

All in all, the war probably changed the United States and Wyoming in less massive and obvious ways than World War II, which isn't to say that it didn't bring about changes. Wyoming was a heavily rural state with a major emphasis on cattle and sheep production before the war, and it still was after. But there were changes. The oil industry, which had been in the state since its onset, really got rolling during World War I in a way that we'd recognize today. It was there prior to the war, and it would have arrived anyhow, but the global demand for oil for vehicles and ships caused the oil industry to leap forward by a decade, if not two, in just a few years. With that, the towns and cities dramatically changed in ways that were permanent for all and still visible in many locations.

November 12

1867 A peace conference commences at Fort Laramie, Wyoming. The goal was to arrive at a peaceful solution to strife between Americans and the northern Plains Indians.

1890 The first Wyoming state legislature is convened.

1890 The United States government funds a land grant college for Wyoming that would become the University of Wyoming.

November 13

1854 The Horse Creek Skirmish occurs when the Sioux attack a mail stage near the present location of Torrington.

1867 The first passenger train, a Union Pacific train, arrives in Cheyenne.

1901 The first CB&Q passenger train arrives in Cody, Wyoming.

November 14

1890 Joseph M. Carey is elected as the first U.S. senator for Wyoming. F.E. Warren is elected as a second senator for Wyoming. At this time, the legislature appointed the senators rather than the electorate electing them.

Carey was an 1864 graduate of the University of Pennsylvania College of Law and became U.S. attorney for the territory of Wyoming in 1869. He was on the Territorial Supreme Court from 1871 to 1876, when he left that field to become a rancher, founding a significant early ranch in Natrona County, Wyoming, the CY. He served as governor from 1890 to 1895, being Wyoming's first state governor, and then again from 1911 to 1915, during which time he supported the Progressive Party campaign for President Theodore Roosevelt.

November 15

1912 The Bishop Randall Hospital is officially opened in Lander, Wyoming.

1921 A truck used by John J. Pershing in the Great War is donated to the Wyoming State Museum.

November 16

1878 The commissary at Fort Fetterman lists the supplies on hand as being 195 pounds of turkey, 140 pounds of codfish and 11 pounds of cherries.

1887 Legendary photographer of Wyoming Charles Belden is born in California.

1942 Wyoming senator Harry H. Schwartz introduces a bill to protect western stockmen from wartime eminent domain losses.

1982 The Jahnke murder occurs in Cheyenne, in which Richard Janke Jr., aided by his sister, kills his abusive father. The murder was later the basis of a television movie entitled *Right to Kill*.

November 17

1906 Eleven people are killed in a head-on train collision near Azusa, Wyoming. The collision was caused by a mistake in a train order in a telegraph, and most of the men killed were railroad employees in a day coach.

November 18

1883 John (Manual Felipe) Phillips (Cardoso) dies in Cheyenne. He is famously remembered as the civilian who rode 236 miles from Fort Phil Kearny to Fort Laramie following the Fetterman fight. Phillips is an interesting character and was born in 1832 in the Azores, which he left at age eighteen on a whaler bound for California in order to pan for gold. He was a gold prospector across the West for fifteen years. He was actually at Fort Phil Kearny as a party of miners he had left pulled into the fort in September 1866. His famous ride is somewhat inaccurately

Portugee Phillips Monument, Johnson County, Wyoming. *Photograph by the author.*

remembered, as he did not make the entire ride alone, as often imagined, but instead rode with Daniel Dixon. Both men were paid $300 for their effort. After this event, Phillips switched occupations to that of mail courier, and then he became a tie hack in Elk Mountain, Wyoming, supplying rails to the Union Pacific. In 1870, he married and founded a ranch at Chugwater, Wyoming. He and his wife sold the ranch in 1878, and he moved to Cheyenne, where he lived until his death.

1890 Francis E. Warren assumes the office of U.S. senator from Wyoming. He was Wyoming's first senator.

1902 Frederick Remington draws pictures of the dedication of Irma Hotel in Cody.

November 19

1909 George Sabin is sentenced for second-degree murder for his part in the Spring Creek Raid. He escaped on December 25, 1913, while on a work gang in Basin and was never recaptured.

The sentencing is remarkable and significant, as it effectively meant an end to private warfare over sheep in Wyoming and also meant that conventional justice had come to the Big Horn Basin, where previously juries would not convict in these circumstances. This reflected in part the horror of the Spring Creek assault but also the fact that the basin was now closer to the rest of the state, having been connected sometime prior by rail.

1980 *Heaven's Gate*, a highly expensive cinematic interpretation of the Johnson County War that was widely panned at the time, premieres. The film has since gained some respect (I've never seen it), but it was not the success hoped for by its makers.

Almost every popular work based on the Johnson County War is a serious failure in some regards, with almost all of them being simplistic in some fashion and failing nearly completely to understand the complexities of what they try to depict. While I have not seen this film and have no real interest in doing so, I would be very surprised if it was much different.

November 20

1903 Tom Horn is hanged for the murder of Willie Nickell.

November 21

1865 Platte Bridge Station is renamed Fort Caspar in honor of the late Caspar Collins, who had lost his life at the Battle of Platte Bridge Station earlier that year.

1895 The Federal District Court, sitting in Cheyenne, holds that the Treaty of 1868 exempted Indians from the state's game laws. The decision would later be reversed.

1940 Ernest Hemingway and Martha Gellhorn are married in Cheyenne. The wedding took place in the Union Pacific Depot dining room.

1950 A DC3 (C-47) airplane crashes into Mount Moran, killing all twenty-one persons on board. The plane was flying in poor weather.

1957 The Department of Defense announces that F.E. Warren AFB will be the nation's first ICBM (Intercontinental Ballistic Missile) base. The base still retains a Strategic Missile Wing today.

November 22

1877 Governor Thayer approves a memorandum to Congress protesting against a proposed division of the Wyoming Territory.

As evident from the various discussions of territorial boundaries found in this book, the boundaries and governmental entities applicable to what is now the state of Wyoming were remarkably fluid up until at least the 1870s.

1889 A fire damages the state capitol.

1982 President Reagan informs Congress of his intent to deploy MX missiles to hardened silos under the command of F.E. Warren AFB.

November 23

1936 Work begins on Wheatland Reservoir #1. Dam construction was a popular Depression-era activity across the western United States not only because of the work it provided and the benefit to agriculture but also because of a belief that projects of this type would help directly beneficially impact the climate.

November 24

1874 Joseph F. Glidden receives his patent for barbed wire. Barbed wire changed the nature of ranching and farming in the West. More than any other single physical item, barbed wire was responsible for the end of the open range and permanently established ranches with fenced pastures. It even changed the nature of the cowboy's work and employment, as it caused the rise of multiple smaller ranches with a small number of year-round employees who worked cattle more and rode less.

1890 Francis E. Warren resigns as governor, a position he held for only a little over a month as state governor but had held for about a year as territorial governor. Nonetheless, he holds the status of being Wyoming's first governor. He resigned in order to take up his duties as a newly elected senator, which, oddly, he had assumed a few days prior to his resignation as governor.

1890 Amos W. Barber assumes the office of governor at age twenty-nine. Barber had not been elected governor but assumed the acting position when Francis E. Warren resigned to assume the office of senator. Barber, who was a surgeon by training and came to Wyoming while serving in the army, would find his term in office plagued by the Johnson County War, during which he was associated with the large stockmen side of the conflict. He is not regarded as a strong governor and probably did not miss the office when he vacated it in 1893. He returned first to the position of secretary of state and then to private medical practice and reentered military service during the Spanish-American War. He later moved to Minnesota but was buried in Cheyenne after his death in Minnesota in 1915.

Barber's time in office was marred by the Johnson County War, and his role in it suggests a potential weakness in his character. On a more positive note, he detected the shenanigans that had occurred with the design of the state's seal and would not tolerate them, although even there he kept his first corrective efforts a secret after the story became controversial.

1929 Senator Francis E. Warren dies. At the time of his death, he had been a senator longer than any other person in U.S. history. He was also the last Union veteran to serve in the U.S. Senate, a distinction in his case that was amplified by the fact that he was a recipient of the Congressional Medal of Honor, which perhaps explains his strong support of the army while a senator. (This might also be explained by the fact that he was John J. Pershing's father-in-law.) He was also the first senator to hire a female secretary. His service was not without some blemishes, as a close association with the large stockmen side of the Johnson County War had given rise to questions about the extent of his association at that time, questions that nearly cost him his political career but quickly passed.

1968 Expedition Island in the Green River is designated a National Historic Landmark. The island is a park in Green River, Wyoming, and marks the location where Major John Wesley Powell began his expedition down the Green River and Colorado River in 1871.

1990 In one of Wyoming's most infamous murder cases, fifteen-year-old James "Jamie" Wiley shoots and kills his stepmother, Becky, and brothers Jesse (age thirteen), Willy (age ten) and Tyrone (age five) and then sets the house on fire.

November 25

1876 The Dull Knife Battle occurs. Colonel Ranald S. Mackenzie, Fourth U.S. Cavalry, in command of Company K, Second U.S. Cavalry; Companies H and K, Third U.S. Cavalry; Companies B, D, E, F, I and M, Fourth U.S. Cavalry; and Companies H and L, Fifth U.S. Cavalry, and accompanied by a large contingent of Pawnees together with Arapaho and even Lakota scouts, surprises the Big Horn mountain camp of Cheyenne under Dull Knife. Sometimes regarded as a somewhat unwarranted attack, Dull Knife's band had been at war with the United States during the preceding summer and had recently attacked and defeated a band of Shoshone. Mackenzie's attack did not succeed in taking the camp whole, but it did succeed in eventually driving out the Cheyenne, who lost a great number of villagers in the frozen retreat thereafter. A large number of the ultimate dead were the old and very young. The attack is remarkable for having occurred in horrific climatic conditions: below zero weather, snow and high winds.

Mackenzie is a figure who tends to be much less remembered in the popular imagination than other Indian War army commanders, but he was actually one of the most effective, and consistently so. He was the son of a career U.S. Navy officer who had risen to the rank of commodore, and his family was very well connected in the military and in politics. Ranald Mackenzie graduated from West Point in 1862 and immediately entered into an army career with, of course, the Civil War raging at that time. During the war, he rose to the rank of brigadier general. He was briefly mustered out of the service at the end of the Civil War but brought back in during Reconstruction as a major general. He thereafter reverted to his permanent rank of captain. During the Indian Wars, he demonstrated tactical and field command brilliance, commanding both infantry and cavalry, as well as black and white troops. During this period, he rose back up to the rank of brigadier general.

Unfortunately, he had begun to decline mentally by the 1870s. This manifested itself as early as the campaign that featured the Dull Knife battle. A poor horseman, he took to the field in terrible conditions with his troops, but in camp, he was already demonstrating signs of mental instability and severe depression. He was ultimately discharged for insanity in 1884, just three years after he purchased a ranch in Texas and had become engaged. He died in 1889 at just forty-eight years of age. The source of his mental decline is not really known and remains somewhat debated today, with a possible head injury being one of the suspected causes.

The following Congressional Medal of Honor would be awarded for action at the Dull Knife fight:

FORSYTH, THOMAS H.: First Sergeant, Company M, Fourth U.S. Cavalry. Place and date: Powder River, Wyoming, November 25, 1876. Citation: "Though dangerously wounded, he maintained his ground with a small party against a largely superior force after his commanding officer had been shot down during a sudden attack and rescued that officer and a comrade from the enemy."

Forsyth was from a wealthy family and was somewhat a man of means, an unusual circumstance for an enlisted man, let alone a career enlisted man. He left the service in 1891, the same year he finally received his Congressional Medal of Honor, at which time he had served in the army for twenty-five years. The retirement period for an army pension at this time was thirty years. He left earlier than the norm for a full retirement, and I suspect that it might have been a medical retirement, which would also have resulted in a pension. He held the rank of first sergeant at the time. He died in 1908 at age sixty-five.

1889 Scarlet fever causes the public school in Rawlins to be closed.

November 26

1984 Big Nose George Parrott's remains are given to the Carbon County Museum.

November 27

1869 The suffrage bill is introduced and passed in the territorial senate.

November 28

Clarence King. *Library of Congress.*

1872 The Diamond Hoax of 1872 is exposed by geologist Clarence King, who issues his opinion that a diamond prospect that had been securing prominent national interest had been salted.

Many wealthy and prominent Americans had been fooled by the scheme and had invested funds to purchase what was thought to be a significant diamond strike. The 1872 date of this event shows the significance that geology had in the state's history from the very onset.

1890 The McKinney Strip contest is settled in favor of Buffalo.

November 29 —
Nellie Tayloe Ross Day

Nellie Tayloe Ross Day is a state holiday in Wyoming, although it is little observed.

1847 Missionaries Dr. Marcus Whitman; his wife, Narcissa; and fifteen others are killed by Cayuse and Umatilla Indians in what is today southeastern Washington, causing the Cayuse War. The Whitmans conducted the first Protestant religious service in Wyoming.

1873 The Laramie County Stockgrowers Association forms in Cheyenne. The organization was one of the precursors of the Wyoming Stock Growers Association.

1876 Nellie Tayloe Ross is born in Missouri.

Nellie Tayloe Ross. This photograph was taken at her farm in Maryland, which she had while working in Washington, D.C. Upon her death, she was buried in Cheyenne. *Library of Congress.*

1901 Mildred Harris, a movie actress, is born in Cheyenne. She was a significant actress in the silent film era, having gone from being a child actor to a major adult actress, but had difficulty making the transition to talking pictures.

Harris is also evidence that, in spite of my notation of changes in moral standards elsewhere, the lives of movie stars have often been as torrid as they are presently. Harris married Charlie Chaplin in 1918, at which time she was seventeen years old and the couple thought, incorrectly, that she was pregnant. She did later give birth during their brief marriage to a boy who was severely disabled and who died

Mildred Harris with Charlie Chaplin. *Library of Congress.*

only three days after being born. The marriage was not a happy one. They divorced after two years, and she would marry twice more. She was married to former professional football player William P. Fleckenstein at the time of her death, a union that had lasted ten years. Ironically, she appeared in three films in 1920, the year of her divorce, as Mildred Harris Chaplin, the only films in which she was billed under that name. While an actress probably mostly known to silent film buffs today, she lived in some ways a life that touched upon many remembered personalities of the era and was also somewhat stereotypically Hollywood. She introduced Edward to Wallis Simpson.

She died in 1944 at age forty-two of pneumonia following surgery. She has a star on the Hollywood Walk of Fame. A significant number of her 134 films have been lost or destroyed due to film deterioration. Her appearances in the last eight years of her life were minor and unaccredited, showing the decline of her star power in the talking era.

Stories like hers, however, demonstrate that the often-held concept of great isolation of Wyomingites was never true. Harris was one of at least three actors and actresses who were born in Wyoming and who had roles in the early silent screen era. Of those, she was arguably the most famous, having risen to the height of being a major actress by age sixteen.

November 30

1803 Spain cedes Louisiana to France, including, of course, the part that is now Wyoming.

1856 Martin's Cove survivors arrive in Salt Lake City.

1869 A woman's suffrage bill is sent to the territorial House.

1920 The Bureau of Reclamation commences construction of an electric power plant at Buffalo Bill Dam.

DECEMBER IN WYOMING

December is a cold month in Wyoming, although not the coldest. At one time, the weather immobilized much of the state, although the hardy residents were ready for the conditions. While today conditions are much different, December weather can still be a challenge, with the state often enduring periods of snow, cold and high winds.

December 1

1869 Uinta County is created by the territorial legislature.

1997 The Wyoming state quarter design is approved.

December 2

1875 A strike at Rock Springs mines, the first for that location, is settled.

1905 A Diamondville mine explosion kills eighteen men.

December 3

1888 Ella Watson applies for the WT brand. Her application was rejected.

1899 A fire at Fort Washakie destroys three buildings. Fort Washakie was still an army-utilized installation at that time, as well as being the seat of government for the Wind River Reservation, which it still is.

December 4

1877 The rail line between Cheyenne and Denver is completed.

1942 Troops arrive at Scottsbluff Army Air Field, a satellite field of the Casper Army Air Field.

December 5

1917 Governor Frank Houx asks for the closing of saloons statewide to regulate alcohol sales as a war measure. Prohibition's fortunes would rise with World War I.

1997 The Wyoming Air National Guard concludes its firefighting duty in Indonesia.

December 6

1866 Colonel Henry B. Carrington and Captain William J. Fetterman are surrounded by Sioux and Cheyenne warriors and engage them briefly before being able to return to Fort Phil Kearny.

1869 A bill on territorial suffrage is amended before passage to grant the franchise at age twenty-one as opposed to eighteen.

December 7

1868 A U.S. post office is reestablished at Green River.

1898 Battery A, Wyoming Light Artillery, arrives in Manila, where it will serve in the Philippine insurrection.

1933 A natural gas explosion at a bank in Torrington kills one and injuries four.

December 8

1868 Crook County is created out of portions of Albany and Laramie Counties.

1869 Territorial governor Campbell approves measures to ask Congress to establish a prison at Laramie and to acquire the location for the prison. The prison still remains in Laramie but as a tourist site. For a while in the late twentieth century, it was used as the University of Wyoming's sheep barn.

1873 A bill is introduced in the territorial legislature to move the capital to Evanston. It failed.

1875 Territorial governor Thayer approves an act creating Pease County, which was later renamed Johnson County.

1941 The FBI warns Japanese residents of Rawlins to be discreet.

December 9

1869 Governor Campbell approves the design for the territorial seal. The seal would continue to be used to some extent after statehood, as the first state seal was subject to extensive controversy as competing senators submitted alternative variants and Governor Barber was left with a mess. This was, moreover, more than a little significant, as during this era state seals were used for national bank notes. Wyoming's, therefore, carried the territorial seal in at least some instances after statehood.

A very fine article on the topic of the state seal appears in the *Annals of Wyoming* 84, no. 2 (Spring 2012) by former geology professor Peter Huntoon.

1873 The territorial legislature approves a measure moving the seat of Sweetwater County from South Pass City to Green River.

1890 A bill for the admission of Idaho and Wyoming as states is introduced into Congress.

December 10—Wyoming Day

1869 Territorial governor John Campbell signs a bill giving full suffrage and public rights to women in Wyoming. This was the first law passed in the United States explicitly granting women the franchise. The bill provided that "every woman of the age of eighteen years residing in this territory, may, at every election cast her vote; and her right to the elective franchise and to hold office under the election laws of the territory shall be the same of electors." Governor Campbell's comment in signing the bill into law was: "I have the honor to inform the Council that I have approved 'An act to grant to the Women of Wyoming Territory the right of Suffrage and to hold office.'"

Critics, or perhaps rather cynics, have sometimes claimed that this served no other purpose other than to raise the number of citizens eligible to vote, thereby increasing the likelihood of early admission as a state, but that view doesn't reflect the early reality of this move. In fact, Wyoming's politicians were notably egalitarian for the time and took women as members of the body politic seriously. During the territorial period, women even served on juries, something that was very unusual in the United States at the time, although they lost this right for a time after statehood.

1869 Territorial school laws go into effect, requiring public schools to be funded by taxation.

1909 Red Cloud (Maȟpíya Lúta)—Oglala Sioux warrior and chief and the only Indian leader to have won a war with the United States in the post-1860 time frame that resulted in a favorable treaty from the Indian perspective— dies at the Pine Ridge Reservation. He was eighty-seven years old, and his fairly long life was not uncommon for Indians of this time frame who were not killed by injuries or disease, showing that the often-cited assumption that people who lived in a state of nature lived short lives is in error. After winning Red Cloud's War, a war waged over the Powder River Basin and the Big Horns, he declined to participate in further wars against the United States, which seems to have been motivated by a visit to Washington, D.C., during which he became aware of the odds against the Plains Indians. He did not become passive and warned the United States that its treatment of Indians on the reservation would lead to further armed conflict, which, of course, was correct.

While his most famous actions are associated with Wyoming, Red Cloud was born in Nebraska, which inducted him in recent years into the Nebraska Hall of Fame.

December 11

1873 The territorial legislature approves the incorporation of Evanston. It would later rescind it and then approve it again.

1875 The territorial legislature appoints a commission to study prison costs in regard to Laramie as the prison location. It determined that cost savings justified appointing the Nebraska penitentiary as the Wyoming territorial prison facility at the time.

December 12

1873 Laramie is incorporated by the territorial legislature.

1910 William Howard Taft nominates Willis Van Devanter to the position of associate justice of the United States Supreme Court.

Van Devanter was born in Indiana and was an 1881 graduate of the Cincinnati Law School. Like many of Wyoming's early political figures, the young Van Devanter saw opportunity in Wyoming and, after obtaining his law degree, relocated to Cheyenne, where he began a significant practice. He served as the chief justice of the Territorial Supreme Court after being appointed to the post at age thirty, and he was chief justice of the Wyoming Supreme Court for four days prior to returning to private practice after Wyoming achieved statehood. During his period of private practice, he was the legal strategist for the large cattlemen following their arrest for the invasion of Johnson County.

In 1896, after becoming afflicted with typhus, he relocated to Washington, D.C. From 1896 to 1900, he served as an assistant attorney general assigned to the Department of the Interior and was a professor at George Washington University's School of Law. In 1903, President Roosevelt nominated him to the Eighth Judicial Circuit Court of Appeals, where he was serving when nominated to the United States Supreme Court. In remarkable contrast to today, his nomination was approved by the Senate on December 15.

1919 Fourteen Spanish flu deaths are reported in Washakie County for this week, which of course occurred during the Spanish flu pandemic. The Spanish influenza was a disaster of epic proportions that managed to impact nearly the entire globe. While accounts vary, some indicate that the flu epidemic first broke out, at least in its lethal form, in Camp Funston, Kansas.

December 13

1873 Governor Campbell approves an act creating Uinta County to build a courthouse and a jail in Evanston. The courthouse remains in that use today and is the oldest courthouse in Wyoming that still serves in its original function. Johnson County's 1884 courthouse is the second oldest.

1879 Pease County is renamed Johnson County.

1913 Lincoln Highway is designated a transcontinental highway, the first to be so designated in the United States.

1913 Yoder is incorporated.

December 14

1877 Cheyenne is incorporated by the territorial legislature.

1914 Grace Raymond Hebard becomes the first woman admitted to the state bar. This was a remarkable achievement in and of itself, but it was only one of a string of such accomplishments made by Hebard. She was also the first woman to graduate from the Engineering Department of the University of Iowa in an era when engineering was an overwhelmingly male profession. She followed this 1882 accomplishment by acquiring an 1885 MA from the same school and then an 1893 PhD in political science from Wesleyan University. She went to work for the State of Wyoming in 1882 and rose to the position of deputy state engineer under legendary state engineer Elwood Mead. She moved to Laramie in 1891 and was instrumental in the administration of the University of Wyoming. She was a significant figure in the suffrage movement and a proponent in Wyoming of Americanization, a view shared by such figures such as Theodore Roosevelt.

She was an amateur historian as well, which is what she is best remembered for today. Unfortunately, her historical works were tinged with romanticism and have not been regarded as wholly reliable in later years. Her history of Sacajawea, which followed thirty years of research, is particularly questioned and would seem to have made quite a few highly romantic erroneous conclusions. On a more positive note, the same impulses led her to be very active in the marking of historic Wyoming trails.

While she was the first woman to be admitted to the Wyoming state bar, she never actually practiced law. Her book collection is an important part of the University of Wyoming's American Heritage Center's collection today.

December 15

1887 The Burlington Northern commences operation on its freight line to Cheyenne.

1890 Burlington Northern commences passenger service between Douglas and Cheyenne. The Douglas depot is now a train museum.

1909 The six-masted schooner *Wyoming*, the largest wooden schooner ever built, is launched in Bath, Maine. The huge schooner was the last one launched on the East Coast of the United States.

1910 Wills Van Devanter is confirmed as a justice of the United States Supreme Court.

1913 George Saban, who had pleaded guilty to second-degree murder in connection with the Spring Creek Raid, escapes while being transported as part of a work detail and is never heard from again.

1919 Wyoming train robber Bill Carlisle is captured after his escape from the state penitentiary. Carlisle is remembered today as a bit of an eccentric who took up train robbery after the era of train robbing had really passed, but his story is much more interesting than just that. He grew up in abject poverty, with both his parents having died when he was young. He wandered into Wyoming in 1915 and took up train robbery the following year. He originally became armed, however, because, as he noted, "you couldn't starve to death in Wyoming if you had a gun with which to shoot game."

After making a fair amount of money in train robbery, he intended to head for Alaska but ended up actually announcing an intent to rob a train on the Union Pacific line by way of a letter to a Denver newspaper. This was done as he learned that others were being arrested for his crimes and he felt badly about that and intended to prove their innocence by publicizing a robbery. He was, however, ultimately arrested and sentenced to life in prison, although his sentence was thereafter shortened to fifty years. However, not wanting to remain in prison effectively for life, he escaped by hiding in a carton of shirts being sent out of the penitentiary.

Shortly after that, he attempted to rob a UP train near Rock River but took little, as the passengers were mostly returning servicemen coming home from World War I and he did not wish to rob them. He was wounded in the robbery and wounded again shortly thereafter when captured.

Upon his return to the penitentiary, he met Father Gerard Schellinger, a Catholic priest who served at Rawlins, and Carlisle experienced a profound religious conversion. He became deeply religious for the rest of his life. He was paroled in 1936 and married later that year, living out the rest of his life until 1964 as a humble reformed man.

December 16

1868 Albany and Carbon Counties are established by the Dakota territorial legislature. At this point in time, Wyoming was part of the Dakota Territory.

1868 The first train, a Union Pacific, arrives at Evanston.

1871 The Wyoming State Library is established.

December 17

1919 Vernon Baker is born in Cheyenne. Baker is a recipient of the Congressional Medal of Honor for his actions in combat in World War I, with his citation reading as follows:

> *For extraordinary heroism in action on 5 and 6 April 1945, near Viareggio, Italy. Then Second Lieutenant Baker demonstrated outstanding courage and leadership in destroying enemy installations, personnel, and equipment during his company's attack against a strongly entrenched enemy in mountainous terrain. When his company was stopped by the concentration of fire from several machine gun emplacements, he crawled to one position and destroyed it, killing three Germans. Continuing forward, he attacked an enemy observation post and killed two occupants. With the aid of one of his men, Lieutenant Baker attacked two more machine gun nests, killing or wounding the four enemy soldiers occupying these positions. He then covered the evacuation of the wounded personnel of his company by occupying an exposed position and drawing the enemy's fire. On the following night Lieutenant Baker voluntarily led a battalion advance through enemy mine fields and heavy fire toward the division objective. Second Lieutenant Baker's fighting spirit and daring*

leadership were an inspiration to his men and exemplify the highest traditions of the Armed Forces.

Baker had a rough start in life, as his parents died while he was still young. Partially raised by his grandparents, he learned how to hunt from his grandfather in order to put meat on the table. Entering the army during World War II, he made the army a career and retired in 1968 as a first lieutenant, his rank at that time reflecting force reductions following World War II. He retired to Idaho, where he chose to live as an avid hunter, and he died there in 2010. Baker is a significant figure from Wyoming not only because he won the Congressional Medal of Honor but also because he was part of Wyoming's small African American community.

December 18

1871 A bill providing for the establishment of Yellowstone National Park is introduced in the U.S. House of Representatives.

1944 The U.S. Supreme Court upholds the wartime internment of U.S. citizens of Japanese extraction, which would, of course, include those interned at Heart Mountain, Wyoming.

December 19

1866 Indians attempt to lure a detachment commanded by Captain James Powell into a trap near Fort Phil Kearny but do not succeed.

1892 A subpoena is issued in the case of *Subpoena, State of Wyoming v. Frank M. Canton, et al.*, a criminal action following the Johnson County War. The original is now held by Texas A&M.

1977 Nellie Tayloe Ross dies at age 101 in Washington, D.C. She was buried alongside her late husband in Cheyenne. She had not, of course, lived in Cheyenne for many years or even for most of her long life. Her years in Washington were considerably longer than those in Wyoming.

December 20

1803 The Louisiana Purchase is completed as the territory is formally transferred from France to the United States during ceremonies in New Orleans. The transfer actually technically also involved Spain but only in some odd jurisdictional sense. Much, but not all, of what would become Wyoming was thereby transferred to the United States, leaving approximately one-third of the state in the hands of Spain and a section of country near what is now Jackson Hole in the Oregon country belonging to the United Kingdom.

While the very early territorial jurisdictions pertaining to Wyoming are now largely forgotten, and while they were always a bit theoretical given the tenuous nature of actual pre–Mexican War control over the territory, there have been six national flags that claimed Wyoming or parts of it: Spain, France, the United Kingdom, Mexico, the Republic of Texas and the United States. With the Louisiana Purchase, France's claim would be forever extinguished, and the majority of what would become the state would belong to the United States.

1812 One of the dates claimed for the death of Sacajawea. If correct, she would have died of an unknown illness at age twenty-four at Fort Manuel Lisa, where it is claimed that she and her husband, Toussaint Charbonneau, were living. If correct, she left an infant girl, Lizette, there, and her son, Jean-Baptiste, was living in a boarding school while in the care of William Clark. Subsequent records support that Charbonneau consented to Clark's adoption of Lizette the following year, although almost nothing is known about her subsequent fate. Jean-Baptiste lived until age sixty-one, having traveled widely and having figured in many interesting localities of the American West.

The 1812 death claim, however, is rejected by the Shoshones, to which tribe she belonged, who maintain that she lived to be nearly one hundred years old and died in 1884 at Fort Washakie, Wyoming. A grave site exists for her, based on the competing claim, in Fort Washakie, the seat of government for the Wind River Reservation. This claim holds that she left Charbonneau and married into the Comanche tribe, which is very closely related to the Shoshone tribe, ultimately returning to her native tribe. This view was championed by Grace Hebard (see December 14), and it even presents an alternative history for Sacajawea's son, Jean-Baptiste, and a second son, Bazil. It was later supported by the conclusions reached by Dr. Charles Eastman, a Sioux physician who was hired by the Bureau of Indian Affairs to research her fate.

While the Wyoming claim is not without supporting evidence, the better evidence would support her death outside Wyoming at an early age. The alternative thesis is highly romantic, which has provided the basis for criticism of Hebard's work. The 1812 date, on the other hand, is undeniably sad, as much of Sacajawea's actual life was. Based on what is now known of her story, as well as the verifiable story of Jean-Baptiste Charbonneau, who traveled in the United States and Europe and held public office in the United States, the Wyoming claim is seriously questionable. That, in turn, leaves the question of the identity of the person buried at Fort Washakie, who appears to have genuinely been married into the Comanche tribe, to have lived to an extremely old age and to have lived a very interesting life, but that identity is unlikely to ever be known or even looked into.

2010 The University of Wyoming puts Bruce Catton's papers online. Catton was a well-known historian of the Civil War.

December 21

Today is the Winter Solstice, the shortest day of the year in the Northern Hemisphere.

1866 A force principally composed of Sioux lures a force principally made up of post–Civil War recruits, commanded by William Fetterman, into an ambush outside Fort Phil Kearny. Fetterman was arrogant in regard to his opinions of his abilities and that of his green troops and insubordinate to some degree in regard to his weak commander, Colonel Carrington. In the resulting battle, Fetterman's entire command of eighty-two (including two civilians) was killed in the largest post–Civil War military disaster of the Indian Wars up until Little Big Horn a decade later. The battle also resulted in a type of siege around Fort Phil Kearny, just a few miles from the battlefield, where the command buttoned up as a result of the disaster.

Coming just a year after the carnage of the Civil War, the defeat, which was recognized as a military disaster at the time, nonetheless did not have the huge public impact that Custer's defeat a decade later in Montana would. Indeed, while recognized as a disaster at the time, the Sioux victory would be a significant battle in Red Cloud's War, the only Plains Indian War won by the Indians.

Like Little Big Horn, the battle has been subjected to continual reinterpretation nearly from the onset. As a recent article in the *Annals of Wyoming* (Spring 2012) reveals, there were "eyewitness" accounts that were fiction from day one, and Colonel Carrington started receiving criticism from the onset. As it turns out, conventional accounts of the battle remain the most accurate, with Carrington urging Fetterman not to go beyond the nearby ridgeline and Fetterman ignoring that order. Fetterman's contempt for his Indian foe that day would prove disastrous.

December 22

1921 President Warren Harding signs an executive order that expands the National Elk Refuge into, additionally, a bird refuge.

December 23

1935 A total of 5,600 jackrabbits are killed in Natrona County in one of the periodic Depression-era rabbit drives that were designed to help feed hungry families. Among the numerous natural disasters inflicted on the nation during the Dust Bowl years were plagues of rabbits.

December 24

1859 The first known lighting of a Christmas tree in Wyoming occurs near Glenrock.

1983 Recluse, Wyoming, sees temperatures of negative fifty-one degrees Fahrenheit, and Echeta sees negative fifty-four degrees.

December 25—Christmas Day

1882 The first recorded turkey dinner in Wyoming takes place at Fort McKinney.

December 26

2008 A swarm of over nine hundred earthquakes occurs in Yellowstone over a wide area. The earthquakes measured up to 3.9 on the Richter Scale. Wyoming is quite tectonically active, and earthquakes are actually quite common in the state.

December 27

1867 The Dakota territorial legislature creates Sweetwater County.

1890 The Union Pacific in Cheyenne receives twelve new switch engines for distribution.

December 28

1883 Lloyd Fredendall is born at Fort D.A. Russell, where his father was then serving. His father was not, however, a career soldier and would later become the Albany County, Wyoming sheriff. Fredendall was twice appointed to West Point by Senator F.E. Warren, being dismissed from the school once for poor academic performance and dropping out once. Nonetheless, he was commissioned into the army after passing a qualifying exam while attending MIT. He served in World War I but did not see combat, as he was assigned to positions in the army's service schools in France.

During World War II, his fortunes rose early, as he was favored by Marshall and liked by Eisenhower, both of whom admired his cocky demeanor. He was assigned to major command positions in Operation Torch but fell out of favor as he was not successful as an actual field commander. He was replaced by Eisenhower following the American defeat at Kasserine Pass and spent the rest of the war in a training command in the United States, where he secured promotion to the grade of lieutenant general. Historians have been hard on him regarding his World War II combat role, proof that he was an inept commander.

December 29

1845 Texas is admitted into the Union. While its borders would soon shrink, at first a small portion of Wyoming previously claimed by Spain, then México and then Texas was within the boundaries of the new state. None of these political entities had actually ever controlled the region, so to some degree, the claim was more theoretical than real.

1916 The Stock Raising Homestead Act of 1916 becomes law. It allowed for 640 acres for ranching purposes but severed the surface ownership from the mineral ownership, which remained in the hands of the United States.

The Stock Raising Homestead Act of 1916 recognized the reality of western homesteading, which was that smaller parcels of property were not sufficient for western agricultural conditions. It was not the only such homestead act, however, and other acts likewise provided larger parcels than the original act, whose 100th anniversary is rapidly coming up. The 1916 act came in the decade that would see the greatest number of homesteads filed nationally.

Perhaps most significant, in some ways, was that the 1916 act also recognized the split estate, which showed that the United States was interested in being the mineral interest owner henceforth, a change from prior policies. The year 1916 was also a boom year in oil and gas production due to World War I, and the United States was effectively keeping an interest in that production. The split estate remains a major feature of western mineral law today.

1931 Sheep Creek stages a rabbit hunt to reduce rabbit numbers and feed the hungry.

1941 All German, Italian and Japanese aliens in California, Idaho, Montana, Nevada, Oregon, Utah and Washington are ordered to surrender contraband.

1941 Sunge Yoshimoto, age nineteen, is killed in the Lincoln-Star Coal Company tipple south of Kemmerer. He was a Japanese American war worker.

December 30

1878 Camp Brown, Wyoming, is renamed Fort Washakie. The change of name is remarkable in that it is the only instance of a frontier army post being renamed in honor of a Native American.

Washakie, who was allied with the United States, figured prominently in Wyoming as a Shoshone scout and was a war leader in both native wars and as the leader of Shoshone war parties in the field in support of the U.S. Army. Washakie had a role in Crook's 1876 expeditions. He would live into the twentieth century, dying in his nineties or one hundreds depending on which birth date is accepted.

December 31

1871 The territorial legislature authorizes the formation of militia companies, the birth of the Wyoming National Guard.

1925 The legendary Swan Land & Cattle Company issues its corporate holdings report for the year.

AFTERWORD

In our daily lives, we move through history unaware of its passing. Sometimes we have a feeling that certain current events are big ones, and every now and then, we become aware that something we're experiencing is historical in nature—but only rarely. In truth, history is the story of our lives. It's much more made up of the daily events of average men and women than it is of extraordinary events put in motion by extraordinary people. Indeed, some of those extraordinary people are extraordinary simply because they became caught up, and therefore known, by extraordinary events.

My hope is that this book helps to convey that a little and helps illustrate a bit of the history of a unique, extraordinary place—Wyoming.

BIBLIOGRAPHY

A Note on the Sources

One of the problems with writing a book the way I wrote this one is that the sources came early and often before I had determined to write a book. Hundreds of books, therefore, could be cited. Books like *Indian Fights and Fighters*, *The Bandetti of the Plains*, *The Last Stand* and many others could, and probably should, be cited. But the way they were used was over a very long time.

Fairly free use has been made of Internet sources, which always have their difficulties but have been checked where possible. Some sources are general rather than specific. Nearly every issue of *Annals of Wyoming* has excellent information on Wyoming in it, and nearly the entire magazine could be cited as a source every issue. *Wyoming Wildlife*, a journal published by the Wyoming Game and Fish Department, also has some surprisingly good historical articles in it, even though this is not the main focus of its efforts.

There are also sources that simply don't show up well in a bibliography. The Wyoming State Historic Preservation Office, for example, has a nice web presence and posts some items of Wyoming's daily history, some of which have ended up in this book. Various odds and ends I ran across here and there, sometimes in newspapers and sometimes in other sources, have ended up here and have not always been noted.

One source that contributed a lot of items was the Wyoming State Historical Society's calendar, which notes something every day. I've used many of these items. Some I did a little research on, and occasionally I found disputes of a day or two in regard to such items. Where that's occurred, I hope I've used the correct date, but of course, there's always the chance I missed the correct date here or there.

Internet Sources

153rd Air Wing History. www.153aw.ang.af.mil/history.
On-This-Day.Com, Today in Wyoming Daily History. www.on-this-day.com/cgi-bin/otd/statesotd/otdWY.pl.
Society of the Military Horse. www.militaryhorse.org.
Today in Old West History. www.knology. net/~lonesomedove/tiowh.html.
Today in Wyoming's History. wyominghistory.blogspot.com.
WyoHistor.Org, a Project of the Wyoming State Historical Society. www.wyohistory.org.
Wyoming State Archives Website. wyoarchives.state.wy.us.

Books

Brooks, Bryant B. *Memoirs of Bryant B. Brooks*. Glendale, CA: Arthur H. Clark Company, 1939.

Cozzens, Peter, ed. *Eyewitness to the Indian Wars, 1865–1890*. Mechanicsburg, PA: Stackpole Books, 2005.

Davis, John W. *Goodbye Judge Lynch*. Norman: University of Oklahoma Press, 2006.

———. *A Vast Amount of Trouble: A History of the Spring Creek Raid*. Norman: University of Oklahoma Press, 2005.

———. *Wyoming Range War*. Norman: University of Oklahoma Press, 2012.

Hunt, Rebecca A. *Natrona County: People, Place and Time*. Virginia Beach, VA: Donning Company Publishers, 2011.

McDermott, John W. *Frontier Crossroads: The History of Ft. Caspar and the Upper Platte Crossing*. Casper: City of Casper, Wyoming, 1997.

Mockler, Alfred James. *History of Natrona County, Wyoming, 1888–1922*. Chicago: R.R. Donnelley & Sons, 1923.

Smith, Helena Huntington. *War on Powder River*. Lincoln: University of Nebraska Press, 1967.

Trumbull, Con, and Kem Nicolaysen. *Casper*. Charleston, SC: Arcadia Publishing, 2013.

Truscott, Lucien. *Twilight of the U.S. Cavalry*. Lawrence: University of Kansas Press, 1989.

Periodicals

Annals of Wyoming. Wyoming State Historical Society.

Casper Star Tribune.

Wyoming State Historical Society Calendar. Wyoming State Historical Society.

ABOUT THE AUTHOR

Patrick T. Holscher was born and grew up in Casper, Wyoming. His parents, Dr. Thomas L. Holscher, DDS, and Patricia U. Holscher, had a deep interest in history of all types, which Pat picked up as a child and carried into adulthood. He graduated from Natrona County High School in 1981 and entered the Third Battalion, Forty-ninth FA, Wyoming Army National Guard, that same year.

Pat attended Casper College, graduating with a degree in geology in 1932, and went on to obtain a BS in geology in 1986. Graduating into one of the state's periodic mineral industry slumps, he then went on to obtain a JD from the University of Wyoming in 1990. He's practiced law in his native Casper since 1990. In his spare time, he subjects his wife, Darcie, and his children, Alexis and Marcus, to lectures and field trips on history.